If spiritual maturity centers on becoming more like Jesus, then grasping how Jesus reflects who God is and how we, like Jesus, are created in God's image seems foundational. Stephen Hiemstra provides a scriptural and accessible introduction to explore these mutually illuminating dynamics for those seeking to explore these central mysteries more fully.

David A. Currie
Professor and Dean
Gordon-Conwell Theological Seminary

Meeting intellectuals where they are, this work communicates a dimension in this world that is usually beyond the reach of the natural mind, except through special revelation.

Annie Hui

Knowing God poses a tough question. Is God in Christ more immanent or transcendent?
Hiemstra expresses God's immanence through fleshy verbs: "Heal ... feed ... confront ... teach ... comfort ... visit ... pray." God's transcendence is more slippery because divinity is a difficult concept to those steeped in a materialistic worldview. If that weren't enough, how do put these attributes together without creating God in our own image?
Hiemstra tackles this task by focusing on the image of God in the person of Jesus.

John A. "Jack" Calhoun
President and CEO, Hope Matters

The *Image of God in the Person of Jesus* is the latest of Stephen Hiemstra's books about the image of God and is the best yet. Well-researched, the book is filled with unexpected details that add to the reader's understanding of the gospels, Paul's message, transcendence, postmodernism, etc. in relation to the Church. Undergirding Hiemstra's scholarly assessment of Jesus as the image of God is his deep well of faith that pours out in the extraordinary prayers that conclude his chapters.

Ann Westerman

In his latest book, *Image of God in the Person of Jesus*, my good friend and author Stephen Hiemstra navigates the complexities of divinity within the context of our human experience. Through reflections on ancient civilizations, biblical narratives, and theological doctrines, Stephen illuminates the enduring significance of God's transcendence in our lives. Delving into topics such as the Apostle's Creed, forgiveness of sins, Old Testament prophecies, and the role of Jesus as both human and divine, Stephen invites us to contemplate the mysteries of our faith.

With clarity and depth, Image of God in the Person of Jesus offers a compelling exploration of the intersection between the divine and the human, inspiring Christians to reflect on their spiritual journey with the Lord.

Eric Teitelman
House of David Ministries

Stephen Hiemstra, in the *Image of God in the Person of Jesus*, writes, "there are no paths up the mountain to God because God, having created time and space, stands outside of both. We cannot approach God; he must approach us and he did so in the person of Jesus of Nazareth." Hiemstra's scholarly research examines extensive sources, from the Bible to Saint Augustine and even the Greek myth of Narcissus, in this lively study of the second person of the Holy Trinity.

Sharron Giambanco
Business owner and writer

What captures seeker attention today is the person and work of Christ. In my seventeen trips to the Middle East, my motivation for going was to visit places where Jesus was born, where He taught, and where He performed miracles. He changed the world. Stephen Hiemstra's work will help you understand and experience more about this Jesus, the person that we call Christ.

Percy M. Burns
Author of Glorious Freedom

Dr. Hiemstra takes us on a tour of the Biblical passages that reveal the image of God shining through the person of Jesus Christ. Some of the sections will surprise you and cause you to wonder, How does this familiar passage reflect the image of God in Jesus? Yet through the author's further explanation, you come to appreciate the breadth and profound depth of the image as it glistens in the prophecies, life and teaching of Jesus. However, it doesn't end there. For as these truths seep into our mind and soul they provide a life-giving perspective that can transform us more and more into this image of our creator.

Rob Bromhead
Pastor Emeritus Centreville Presbyterian Church

Image of God in the Person of Jesus is the last in Stephen Hiemstra's Image of God series and rightfully so. In Jesus we see the culmination of God's plan for humanity, His mercy and saving grace. Stephen's careful and thoughtful approach to the person of Jesus, totally human but at the same time totally divine is compelling for the believer as well as the non-believer. Stephen uses a very logical pathway to present the person of Jesus, from the prophecies in the Old Testament to His resurrection in the New Testament. Make sure you do not skip the Conclusion section where Stephen brings it all together in the topic of the Trinity.

This series lends itself to be used as a personal devotional guide or as a group study. The questions at the end of each chapter help you ensure that you pondered and understood the material presented. But my all time favorite section is the prayer. These prayers are not only profound but they put into words thoughts and doubts I have had and did not know how to express.

May the Lord richly bless you as you delve into this book and learn about who Jesus is and what He has done for you.

Nohemi Zerbi
Commissioned Lay Pastor
First Presbyterian Church of Greenback, TN

Is there anything less suited to our Postmodern world than the Jesus the first Christian's encountered—a Divine rescuer, breaking through the bounds of space and time? Jesus the ancient rabbi shepherding his small flock of followers seems easier to believe and less challenging to follow. (but) What if Jesus was actually both these things? And what if this Jesus is the one we actually need? Through deep scholarship, guided prayer and introspective questions Stephen Hiemstra offers us a path back to the Jesus who was and is and will be forever.

Aaron McMillan
Pastor

OTHER BOOKS BY THE AUTHOR

Image of God Series:

Image of God in the Parables

Image of the Holy Spirit and the Church

Image of God in the Person of Jesus

Christian Spirituality Series:

A Christian Guide to Spirituality[1]

Life in Tension

Called Along the Way[2]

Simple Faith

Living in Christ

Image and Illumination

Masquerade Series:[3]

Masquerade

The Detour

Christmas in Havana

Prayerbooks:

Everyday Prayers for Everyday People

Prayers[4]

Prayers of a Life in Tension

---

1 Also available in Spanish and German.
2 Also available in Spanish.
3 Screenplays have been adapted from these books.
4 Also available in Spanish.

IMAGE OF GOD IN THE PERSON OF JESUS

Forgotten Path in Winter

IMAGE OF GOD IN THE PERSON OF JESUS

Stephen W. Hiemstra

T2P

T2Pneuma Publishers LLC
Centreville, Virginia

IMAGE OF GOD IN THE PERSON OF JESUS

Copyright © 2024 Stephen W. Hiemstra
ISNI: 0000-0000-2902-8171, All rights reserved.

With the exception of short excerpts used in articles and critical reviews, no part of this work may be reproduced, transmitted, or stored in any form whatsoever, printed or electronic, without prior written permission of the publisher.

T2Pneuma Publishers LLC
P.O. Box 230564, Centreville, Virginia 20120
www.T2Pneuma.com

Names: Hiemstra, Stephen W., author.
Title: Image of God in the person of Jesus / Stephen W. Hiemstra. Series: Image of God
Description: Includes bibliographical references and index. | Centreville, VA: T2Pneuma Publishers LLC, 2024.
Identifiers: LCCN: 2024903643 | ISBN: 978-1-942199-61-8 (paperback) | 978-1-942199-95-3 (KDP) | 978-1-942199-83-0 (epub)
Subjects: LCSH Jesus Christ. | Jesus Christ--Humanity. | God (Christianity) | God--Attributes. | BISAC RELIGION / Christian Living / Devotional | RELIGION / Faith | RELIGION / Christian Living / Spiritual Growth
Classification: LCC BT218 .H54 2024 | DDC 232.8--dc23

Many thanks to my editors, Jean Arnold and Sarah Hamaker, for their prompt and precise work. Thanks also to my readers, Annie Hui and Nathan Snow, for their helpful comments..

All Scripture quotations, unless otherwise indicated, are taken from The Holy Bible, English Standard Version, Copyright © 2000; 2001 by Crossway Bibles, a division of Good News Publishers. Used by permission. All rights reserved.

Cover art by C. Hiemstra (2024), *Joshua*, Used with Permission.
Cover by SWH

CONTENTS

PREFACE.. vii

INTRODUCTION

Transcendence...3
Old Testament... 10
The Apostle Paul... 15
The Gospels... 21
Hebrews..26

THE TRANSCENDENCE CHALLENGE

Self-Awareness.. 33
The Self-Referencing Problem................................. 40
Small-T Transcendence.. 46
Large-T Transcendence.. 51
Healing Ministry... 57

OLD TESTAMENT PROPHECIES

The Mission... 65
Messiah Described... 71
New Covenant... 78
The Story of Isaac..85
Christ Figures.. 91

THE APOSTLE PAUL

Paul's Conversion...99
Primacy of Divinity.. 105
Paul's Ministry Partners.. 109
Gospel Timing...115

THE GOSPELS

The Context..121
Jesus' Early Life.. 129
The Lost Years...135
Available, Ask, Articulate....................................... 141
Emotional Intelligence... 146

(GOSPELS continued)

Scandalous Engagement 152
Jesus' Young Life 156
Pastoral Care 162
Gethsemane 167
Jesus' Final Hours 172
The Risen Christ 178

CONCLUSIONS

Trinity 187
The Template 197
Image of God 203

SCRIPTURAL INDEX 207
REFERENCES 213
ABOUT 223

PREFACE

I was sent only to the lost sheep of the house of Israel.
(Matt 15:24)

The postmodern church struggles to understand Jesus. This struggle can be a genuine attempt to know God better, or it can be an insidious attempt to create God in our own image. Is Jesus more immanent (human) or transcendent (divine)? Who is he?

The first book written in the New Testament is likely the Apostle Paul's Letter to the Church at Thessalonica.[1] This implies that in a literary sense the Apostle Paul is the father of the New Testament. Paul only knew the Risen Christ, which implies that for him the divinity of Christ was obvious. The Gospels that record the humanity of Christ were written almost a generation later. The transcendence problem facing postmodern people that fixates on the humanity of Christ is something new.

My recent book, *Image and Illumination* (2023), focused on Christian anthropology, asking the question: What does it mean to be created in the image of God? Embedded in this question is the metaphysical question: Who

---

[1] Scholars debate whether the first book was Thessalonians or Galatians. The image of Jesus presented is the same in both books.

is God? The New Testament addresses this question with three pictures of God: The person of Jesus, Jesus' teaching about God the Father in the parables, and the founding of the church on Pentecost by the Holy Spirit. In this book, I focus on the *Image of God in the Person of Jesus*.

Transcendence Challenge

Postmodern people live in a materialist world, where the only things thought to exist are those that we can touch, taste, smell, hear, or see. Because God lies outside the physical universe of the materialist, he is defined as nonexistent. The materialist worldview works like an invisible dog fence to restrict our imagination. Postmodern people are transcendence-challenged making it hard to believe that Jesus is both human and divine.

To get beyond this limitation, it is helpful to distinguish three definitions of transcendence.

The first is most generic and includes anything not material—anything immaterial, conceptual, or spiritual—such as God's self-revelation to Moses: "The LORD, the LORD, a God merciful and gracious, slow to anger, and abounding in steadfast love and faithfulness." (Exod 34:6) How can you touch mercy? What does grace look like? What about patience, love, and faithfulness? A scientist cannot measure any of these attributes, yet they are as important to life as the nose on your face.

Second, anything outside the natural world—the supernatural, the miraculous—is transcendent.

Finally, anything set apart—holy—is transcendent. The first sentence in the Bible gives two aspects of this class of transcendence: "In the beginning, God created the heavens and the earth." (Gen 1:1) Because God created both time and space, he transcends both. Jeffrey Niehaus (2017, 70) observes that "Since God is outside time, he can foreknow exactly what may be future in a human timeline, because for him it is at once future, present, and past" (Rom 8:29).

Old Testament Prophecies

Prophecies of a messiah to come run throughout the Old Testament in both the law and the prophets. In Genesis 3:15 we read: "I will put enmity between you [Satan] and the woman [Eve], and between your offspring and her offspring; he shall bruise your head, and you shall bruise his heel." Some read this first mention of a messiah as prophesying spiritual war ending with Satan's defeat. Later in Job, we read: "For I know that my Redeemer lives, and at the last he will stand upon the earth." (Job 19:25) A redeemer is, among other things, someone who ransoms prisoners taken as slaves in war. Thus, when Jesus died on the cross to pay the penalty for our sin (e.g. 1 Cor 15:3), he functioned as a redeemer.

The Old Testament prophecy most prominently featured in the New Testament is found in Isaiah 61:1: "The Spirit of the Lord GOD is upon me, because the LORD has anointed me to bring good news to the poor." Jesus cited this passage in both his call sermon in Luke 4 and in the Beatitudes introducing the Sermon on the Mount (Matt 5:1–10). This passage is accordingly in view as Jesus ministered to the lost sheep of Israel (Matt 15:24). These prophecies tie Jesus' ministry to the story of Israel and validate the New Testament claim that Jesus is both human (born in time to a real mother) and divine (able to serve as an acceptable sacrifice for sin).

The Pauline Letters

In Paul's first letter to the church at Thessalonica, the first mention of Jesus reads:

> For they themselves report concerning us the kind of reception we had among you, and how you turned to God from idols to serve the living and true God, and to wait for his Son from heaven, whom he raised from the dead, Jesus who delivers us from the wrath to come. (1 Thess 1:9–10)

Paul makes three interesting points in this first mention of Jesus: Jesus was raised from the dead, is the son of God, and serves as a deliverer, which is a synonym for redeemer. Critics often question whether the New Testament claims Jesus to be divine. Here being the son of heaven and possessing the ability to forgive sins both sound divine.

If the earliest letter of Paul makes a claim of divinity, it struck a tone and set the theme for things written and experienced later. Like Paul, we only know the Risen Christ.

The Gospels

The Gospels often get more attention than the letters of Paul, but they were likely finalized decades later. Journalist Lee Strobel (2005, 31) reports: "The standard scholarly dating, even in very liberal circles, is Mark in the 80s, Matthew and Luke in the 80s, John in the 90s." This conclusion may be scholarly error, however, because most authors edit important manuscripts over years before publishing them to the world. Mark, who is thought to have written the first Gospel account, traveled with Paul telling the Jesus story because he served as a scribe to the Apostle Peter and because Paul was himself a late convert, not a disciple. An early draft of his Gospel (often called Q, short for the German word, *Quelle*, that means source) may have already been in use even when Paul himself was evangelizing and writing letters.

As explicit biographies, the Gospels give us a better picture of the humanity of Jesus. The suffering of Jesus on the cross was not his only suffering. Jesus was picked on by his critics, that is bullied, because of his parentage (Mary and Joseph were not married at his conception), humble background (nursed in a manger, raised in Nazareth), and unworthy disciples (fishermen). Even if he was a gifted child, Jesus' suffering was real and his life story clearly shows how God can raise the most humble above their afflictions and provide hope.

The Early Church

The Book of Acts provides numerous ancient sermons whose primary content was the story of Jesus. Consider Peter's sermon on Pentecost:

> Men of Israel, hear these words: Jesus of Nazareth, a man attested to you by God with mighty works and wonders and signs that God did through him in your midst, as you yourselves know—this Jesus, delivered up according to the definite plan and foreknowledge of God, you crucified and killed by the hands of lawless men. (Acts 2:22–23)

What is so striking about this sermon is that it was preached in Jerusalem before an audience of eye-witnesses. No one could dispute the truth of what was said because they themselves had seen it, and three thousand people had a come-to-Jesus moment after this sermon (Acts 2:41).

Christian Spirituality

The unity of immanence and transcendence in Christ shows up in discussions of heart and mind. The Hebrew unity of heart and mind poses a special challenge in today's world where heart and mind are frequently treated as separate with one or the other being emphasized—a Greek, not a Hebrew, idea. Neglect of the heart leads to a stale, distant faith, while neglect of the mind leads to a superficial faith with little application to daily challenges. The image of a Triune God—Father, Son, and Holy Spirit—reminds us that heart and mind are best considered together.

Image of God and the Person of Jesus is the third and final book in my Image of God series. The first book, *Image of God in the Parables*, studies the image of God the Father found in Jesus' parables. The second book, *Image of the Holy Spirit and the Church*, focuses on the role of the Holy Spirit and the church. This book is written in a devotional format with a reflection, prayers, and questions for study. Because the questions have been developed to enhance understanding of the reflection, some readers have started their devotions by reviewing the questions.

Soli Deo Gloria

∞

Blessed Lord Jesus,

All praise and honor, power and dominion, truth and justice are yours because you ransomed us through your life, death, and resurrection. Because you first loved us, humanity flowered and our lives have intrinsic value.

We confess that we have followed your example lightly or not at all. We are shattered images undeserving of your love and attention.

Thank you for your love, both unconditional and conditional, loving us better than our own mothers and fathers, in spite of our rebellious nature and broken faith.

In the power of your Holy Spirit, break every chain with which Satan binds us, be it traumatic pain, impious griefs, blistering illnesses, or soul-crushing addictions. Come in our hearts and cleanse us of all such sin, transgressions, and iniquities that we might be whole again. Give us hearts and minds for you alone, and Christian friends and a faithful church to aid us in life's journey.

In the name of the Father, the Son, and the Holy Spirit, Amen.

∞

Questions
1. What is the difference between immanence and transcendence? Why do we care?
2. What are three definitions of transcendence? Why is it important that Jesus is divine?
3. What was Jesus' mission? What Old Testament passage best defined his approach to that mission?
4. What does redemption mean? Why do we care?

INTRODUCTION

2 – *Image of God in the Person of Jesus*

Transcendence

> *I am the Alpha and the Omega, says the Lord God, who is and who was and who is to come, the Almighty.*
> (Rev 1:8)

Defining transcendence as immaterial, supernatural, and/or holy allows us to begin exploring the nature of divinity in the Bible. It is hard to discuss a topic when the words employed are unclear or ill-defined. It is even harder to believe something that is far removed from our normal experience, vocabulary, or purview.

Transcendence as a Reflection of Life

The ancient Egyptians helped define our understanding of divinity and life everlasting because their daily life was so miserable. Life expectancy was short because food supplies were unreliable, diseases incurable, and common problems, like intestinal parasites (e.g. Acts 12:23), were extremely painful. Infant mortality was so bad that children were not even named until they were a couple years old. Daily life was so miserable—even for the wealthiest—that the ancient Egyptians obsessed about the after-life.

A contrast can be drawn here to postmoderns for whom food is ever-available, many diseases can be mitigated, and life expectancy is more than double that of ancient times. Daily life for most people is at least tolerable and the wealthy seem to have it easy. In this new context, many people have forgotten about God and only joke about the after-life, displaying little fear of divine judgment. Nevertheless, for the world's poor the reality of God remains palpable.

What do you do when a pandemic arises and you have no access to vaccines and modern medicine? The answer today is the same as in ancient times. You pray to God.

The Apostle's Creed

The most of recorded history, people have accepted the transcendence of God. Consider the Apostle's Creed written in Greek circa AD 341 and still memorized by many Christians today:

> I believe in God, the Father Almighty,
> creator of heaven and earth.
> I believe in Jesus Christ, his only begotten son, our Lord,
> who was conceived by the Holy Spirit
> and born of the Virgin Mary.
> He suffered under Pontius Pilate,
> was crucified, died, and was buried;

> He descended to hell. The third day He rose again from the dead.
>
> He ascended to heaven and is seated at the right hand of God the Father Almighty.
>
> From there he will come to judge the living and the dead.
>
> I believe in the Holy Spirit,
>
> the holy Catholic Church,
>
> the communion of saints,
>
> the forgiveness of sins;
>
> the resurrection of the body,
>
> and the life everlasting. Amen.[1]

While eight of the sixteen statements here focus on Jesus and his life story, even more—all but three (6, 7, and 12)—of these statements require a form of transcendence. Four of the five fundamentals of faith—biblical inerrancy, the divinity of Jesus Christ, his virgin birth, resurrection of Christ, and his return—required for ordination in the Presbyterian church in 1910 and struck from requirement in 1925 (Longfield 1991, 161) require transcendence and come from the Apostle's Creed.

In striking the fundamentals of the faith in 1925, the church highlighted the newness of transcendency problem that has been a product of Enlightenment thinking

---
[1] The references to the Apostle's Creed are all taken from FACR (2013, Q/A 23). Another translation is found in (PCUSA 1999, 2.1—2.3).

since the nineteenth century. The doctrine of biblical inerrancy, which required scripture be literally true, upgraded the earlier concept of biblical infallibility that only required the Bible's sufficiency in matters of salvation. This upgrade strived to ameliorate the transcendency problem posed by the debate over evolution and creation, but it really only raised the temperature of the debate without dealing the merits.

Forgiveness of Sins

The problem of sin arose in the Garden of Eden when God put only one requirement on Adam:

> And the LORD God commanded the man, saying, You may surely eat of every tree of the garden, but of the tree of the knowledge of good and evil you shall not eat, for in the day that you eat of it you shall surely die. (Gen 2:16–17)

Death was a divine curse for this original sin. "There is none who does good" (Ps 53:1). A divine penalty attached to a divine stipulation. Sin was a rebellion against God himself. Only God himself could reverse the curse and forgive sins (e.g. Mark 2:7).

The costly nature of redemption is discussed when the psalmist writes: "Truly no man can ransom another, or give to God the price of his life, for the ransom of their life is costly and can never suffice, that he should live on forever and never see the pit." (Ps 49:7–9) But, God himself promises to redeem us (Ps 49:15).

The idea that Jesus died on the cross to redeem us from sin is well-attested in the New Testament (e.g. Matt 1:21; 1 Thess 1:9–10; 1 Cor 15:3)—a doctrine that is often referred to as the atonement. The Apostle Paul explained the atonement as a reversal of Adam's sin. Adam was sinless until he disobeyed God in the Garden of Eden; Jesus was sinless, and he obeyed God to the point of death on a cross. The resurrection credentialed Jesus as divine, making his sacrifice sufficient to reverse the curse of death brought about by the first Adam's sin and prophesied in Isaiah 53:12 (Lindsey 1985, 4–6).

This is why Paul could observe that "If Christ has not been raised, your faith is futile and you are still in your sins." (1 Cor 15:17) This syllogism bears repeating. No resurrection; no divinity, no atonement. You are unforgiven and still under law, not Gospel. Claiming the name of a dead—merely human—martyr cannot reverse the divine penalty for sin.

Transcendence is a critical insight in the Gospel

presented in the New Testament, and it is reflected in the Apostle's Creed adopted by the early church. Today's transcendence problem is not a trivial matter. It lies at the heart of the Gospel as articulated by the Apostle Paul.

∞

Almighty Father,

All praise and honor, power and dominion, truth and justice are yours because you sent Jesus to live among us, to die on the cross, and to be raised from the dead to atone for our sins. Thank you, Jesus!

Forgive our hardened hearts that have relished sin, transgressed your law, and practiced iniquity without bounds. Soften our hearts.

Thank you for first loving us that we might be forgiven and approach you as children approach their good fathers. Do not become impatient with us.

In the power of your Holy Spirit, draw us to yourself: Open our hearts, illumine our thoughts, and strengthen our hands in your service, today and always, that we might rest with you.

In Jesus' precious name, Amen.

∞

Questions
1. What are three definitions of transcendence?
2. How have life experiences changed our attitude about transcendence?
3. How does the Apostle's Creed inform our understanding of Jesus and transcendence?
4. What syllogism does the Apostle Paul use to discuss forgiveness of sin?

Old Testament

> *The heavens declare the glory of God,*
> *and the sky above proclaims his handiwork.*
> *Day to day pours out speech,*
> *and night to night reveals knowledge.*
> (Ps 19:1–2)

God reveals himself to humanity through general and special revelation. General revelation reveals his existence while special revelation reveals his character. When you feel close to God in nature or music, you are talking about general revelation, but God's character is revealed primarily through scripture.

These distinctions are helpful in understanding Old Testament expectations and prophecies concerning Jesus as messiah. A messiah is someone who has been anointed with oil: Priests, prophets, and kings. The New Testament Greek term for messiah is Christ.

Salvation

Salvation in the Old Testament is pictured primarily as a physical, not a spiritual, concept. The Exodus is a story of God's salvation of the people of Israel from slavery in Egypt, which has been retold many times in the Old Testament (e.g. Ps 105) as in Isaiah:

But now thus says the LORD, he who created

> you, O Jacob, he who formed you, O Israel: Fear not, for I have redeemed you; I have called you by name, you are mine. When you pass through the waters, I will be with you; and through the rivers, they shall not overwhelm you; when you walk through fire you shall not be burned, and the flame shall not consume you. For I am the LORD your God, the Holy One of Israel, your Savior. I give Egypt as your ransom, Cush and Seba in exchange for you. (Isa 43:1–3)

Here the crossing of the Red Sea and the Jordan River is retold in a generic form suggesting a spiritual truth, but it is expressed as a concrete, physical event.

This salvation occurs in a pattern outlined in Deuteronomy 30:1–3 that Brueggemann (2016, 59) describes as the Deuteronomic Cycle. Here the pattern is collective sin, scattering and enslavement, crying out to the Lord, and the sending of a deliverer. This pattern is repeated throughout the Old Testaments, but especially in the Book of Judges.

Christ Figures

The Deuteronomic Cycle culminates with God's sending of a deliverer. The Old Testament has many such deliverers—figures such as Joseph, Moses, Joshua, David, and even a gentile, Cyrus king of Persia, who rebuilt Jerusalem (Ezr 1:1). The common characteristic of these deliverers was charismatic leadership.

Genealogies

A key prophecy of Christ is given in God's covenant with David:

> The LORD declares to you that the LORD will make you a house. When your days are fulfilled and you lie down with your fathers, I will raise up your offspring after you, who shall come from your body, and I will establish his kingdom. He shall build a house for my name, and I will establish the throne of his kingdom forever. (2 Sam 7:11–13)

The word, house, can mean both a building and a dynasty. The inference here is that David will begin a dynasty that will live in perpetuity. A dynasty is itself a statement about a human family, but the idea of an everlasting kingdom suggests divinity, which Psalm 110 appears to reiterate. The genealogies of the New Testament in Matthew 1 and Luke 3, like the Old Testament genealogies before them, are normally interpreted as a king list that indicates a dynasty.

Servant Songs

Jesus took the text of his call sermon (Luke 4) and a portion of the Sermon on the Mount (Matt 5) from Isaiah 61. The influence of Isaiah on Jesus' ministry is enormous. Consider these verses:

> There shall come forth a shoot from the stump of Jesse, and a branch from his roots shall bear fruit. And the Spirit of the LORD shall rest upon him, the Spirit of wisdom and understanding, the Spirit of counsel and might, the Spirit of knowledge and the fear of the LORD. (Isa 11:1–2)

This messianic prophecy anticipated Jesus' birth and character. Jesse was King David's father, and Jesus came from the house of David.

Isaiah's influence evokes a tension between the expectation of a charismatic military leader and the humble person that Jesus was. As we read:

> He was despised and rejected by men, a man of sorrows and acquainted with grief; and as one from whom men hide their faces he was despised, and we esteemed him not. (Isa 53:3)

This tension runs throughout the four Servant Songs of Isaiah: Isaiah 42:1–9; 49:1–13; 50:4–11; 52:13–53:12 (e.g. Oswalt 2003, 45; Lindsey 1985, 3). These divergent trends in the Old Testament suggest that Jesus, both as a human and divine person, is a much more complex figure than anyone anticipated.

∞

Almighty and Loving Father,

All praise and honor, power and dominion, truth and justice are yours because you drew yourself to us in your creation and introduced us to your character in your scripture that we might see you face to face in the person of Jesus.

Forgive our unwillingness to listen, read, and study your word or emulate your example in Jesus of Nazareth.

Thank you for your mercy, grace, patience, loving kindness, and faithfulness (Exod 34:6).

In the power of your Holy Spirit, remove the scales from our eyes and the wax in our ears that we might learn to love good things and follow the example of your son, our Lord, Jesus Christ.

In Jesus' precious name, Amen.

∞

Questions
1. What is the difference between general and special revelation?
2. What was the nature of salvation in the Old Testament?
3. What is the Deuteronomic Cycle, and what is a Christ figure?
4. What is a messiah?
5. What tension do we see in the Book of Isaiah with respect to our expectation of a messiah?

The Apostle Paul

> *Go, for he is a chosen instrument of mine
> to carry my name before the Gentiles and kings
> and the children of Israel.
> For I will show him how much
> he must suffer for the sake of my name.*
> (Acts 9:15–16)

*T*he Apostle Paul wrote first about Jesus, yet he only knew the Risen Christ. He grew up in Tarsus in Asia Minor, not in Jerusalem or Galilee like Jesus' other disciples, and he was an early persecutor of the church. Yet, he became the template for Christian converts, and his conversion story appears three times in the Book of Acts (Acts 9:1–20, 22:4–21, 26:9–23). Because he was a highly educated Jew, he knew the Old Testament better than any of the apostles and wrote more than half of the New Testament. Without Paul, the divinity of Christ may not have been clearly articulated, and Christianity may have remained merely a sect in the Jewish faith.

Paul's Conversion

Before his conversion, Paul was known by his Jewish name, Saul of Tarsus. He was a student of Gamaliel, who was a member of the Council of the Pharisees (Acts 5:34; 22:3), which would make Paul one of the best-educated and best-connected men in Israel at the time. Paul would have fit the profile of the rich young ruler (e.g. Luke 18:18–23). His hometown of Tarsus in Asia Minor in modern-day Turkey is important because Paul was familiar with the region and local customs when he traveled there on his first missionary trip.

The first mention of Saul in the Book of Acts is during the stoning of Stephen: "Then they cast him out of the city and stoned him. And the witnesses laid down their garments at the feet of a young man named Saul." (Acts 7:58) Saul not only approved of Stephen's stoning, he went on to lead the subsequent persecution of the church: "But Saul was ravaging the church, and entering house after house, he dragged off men and women and committed them to prison." (Acts 8:2–3) Note the word ravage—Saul was enthusiastic in his persecution.

A key verse in understanding the church's development is:

> But you will receive power when the Holy Spirit has come upon you, and you will be my witnesses in Jerusalem and in all Judea and Samaria, and to the end of the earth. (Acts 1:8)

Even in his persecution of the church, Saul could not help

but advance the Gospel: "Now those who were scattered went about preaching the word." (Acts 8:4) When Jesus appeared to Saul on the road to Damascus, the Gospel had already been preached in Judea and Samaria. After his encounter with the Risen Christ, only days later Saul preached the Gospel in the Synagogue in Damascus, and the Jews plotted to kill him (Acts 9:20, 24).

Paul as Apostle

The dramatic nature of Paul's conversion begs the question of how it happened. The only people to evangelize Paul were those he arrested and threw in prison, except for Stephen. Paul must have heard Stephen's testimony before the Sanhedrin (Acts 7). The key verses in Stephen's testimony were:

> Heaven is my throne, and the earth is my footstool. What kind of house will you build for me, says the Lord, or what is the place of my rest? Did not my hand make all these things?' You stiff-necked people, uncircumcised in heart and ears, you always resist the Holy Spirit. As your fathers did, so do you. Which of the prophets did your fathers not persecute? And they killed those who announced beforehand the coming of the Righteous One, whom you have now betrayed and murdered. (Acts 7:49–52)

The kicker for the Sanhedrin was the charge: "What kind

of house will you build for me?" Things made by the hand of men is code language for idolatry. Restricting worship to the temple was the source of income for the priests and high priests that populated the Sanhedrin. This implies that Stephen's criticism was more than a theological debating point; it threatened their livelihood.

The words of Christ on the Road to Damascus echo Stephen's charge of persecuting the prophets:

> Now as he went on his way, he approached Damascus, and suddenly a light from heaven shone around him. And falling to the ground, he heard a voice saying to him, Saul, Saul, why are you persecuting me? And he said, Who are you, Lord? And he said, I am Jesus, whom you are persecuting. (Acts 9:3–5)

Paul's experience echoes the call of the Prophet Ezekiel (Eze 1:27–28). Significantly, Paul's commission to evangelize the Gentiles appears in all three accounts of his conversion.

Paul's Example

Paul's sensitivity to the Holy Spirit and vast knowledge of scripture have blessed the church with a much deeper understanding of Jesus' humanity and his divinity. Head and heart go hand-in-hand in Paul's writing.

Immanence and Transcendence

Paul serves as a template for the modern Christian. Paul is the only first-century disciple who claims apostleship based solely on a vision of the Risen Christ. Luke records that in replacing Judas Iscariot, the disciples considered two men, Barsabbas called Justus and Matthias (Acts 1:23), as suitable to replace him as an apostle because they had both been with Jesus and had witnessed the resurrection (Acts 1:21–22). Because Paul was the first to write about Jesus in the New Testament, he must have influenced other disciples to record their experiences.

Paul did not meet Luke's criteria for an apostle, but neither do we. Our only first-hand experience of Jesus is with the Risen Christ.

∞

Almighty Father,

All praise and honor, power and dominion, truth and justice are yours because you meet us in our daily lives and encourage us to look beyond the mundane to the transcendent.

Forgive us for our limited vision, our unwillingness to stretch ourselves, and become the persons that you would have us be. For your will for us many times is to make better decisions, not to wait for comfortable, risk-free answers.

Thank you for the example of the Apostle Paul who, though a persecutor of the church, was willing to listen for the voice of God and to learn from his mistakes.

In the power of your Holy Spirit, be ever with us. Calm our nerves. Grant us wisdom beyond our years. May we ever look to you in our distress.

In the precious name of Jesus, Amen.

∞

Questions
1. How did Paul come to faith in Jesus Christ?
2. What verse is the key to understanding Paul's being led by the Holy Spirit?
3. Why was Paul different than other apostles?
4. How did Paul contribute to our understanding of the Jesus story?

The Gospels

> *I will put enmity between you and the woman,*
> *and between your offspring and her offspring;*
> *he shall bruise your head, and you shall bruise his heel.*
>
> (Gen 3:15)

Jerome Neyrey (1998, 1–2) writes in his commentary on the Gospel of Matthew: "The Gospels follow in great measure conventional formulas for praise articulated in the epideictic rhetoric [a kind of oral obituary] of praise and in the rules for the *encomium*." The form of an *encomium* in the Greco-Roman context appears in a handbook known as a *progymnasmata*, which is like a school book for students of rhetoric. An *encomium* must include all aspects of a hero's life (birth, education and training, public and death) and is particularly important in an honor-shame culture (Neyrey 1998, 11). You don't really know a person until you have attended their funeral because of the testimonials that are given.

The Gospels introduce us to the humanity of Jesus by telling his life story, teaching, interaction with other celebrities, death, and resurrection. They are not a typical *encomium* because Jesus rose from the dead. Nevertheless, the Jesus' divinity breaks through in his life through his healings, signs, wonders, and exorcisms. These are all miraculous and point beyond his life to God and Jesus' divinity. The implication is that the humanity and the divinity of Jesus are commingled throughout his life.

An audience today would want to know more about Jesus than the Bible records. We know nothing about his personal appearance, education, acquaintances, preferences, or language abilities. We are told that he grew up in Nazareth, was conceived out of wedlock, was an ethnic Jew, his family was poor, and he worked as a carpenter (Mark 6:3).

Each of these details pose interesting questions. For example, Nazareth in Galilee lay within walking distance of Sepphoris, a city with a Greek theater burned to the ground in 4 BC following a Jewish revolt against the Herodians (Thurman 1996, 18). Was Jesus a rube—a poor, country bumpkin—as often alleged since the Scope trial in 1925 or was he something more? Jesus' social position rides on answers to such questions. Yet often the Gospels do not provide us with clear answers.

Relationship among the Gospels

Throughout the history of the church, the Gospel of Matthew was thought to have been the first to be written. Scholars began in the nineteenth century to argue that the Gospels of Matthew and Luke displayed a literary dependence on the Gospel of Mark with common passages being described as part of an unretained Q document. Because of the common themes and passages Matthew, Mark, and Luke are often described as the synoptic Gospels, while the Gospel of John appears independent of the others.

The uplifting, spiritual nature of John's Gospel led some early church writers to describe John's Gospel as "The Eagle" (Rev 12:14). It is John's Gospel that gives us a picture of Jesus offering one-on-one pastoral care and the only obvious sermon series in scripture—the "I AM" discourses. The synoptic Gospels provide us with more of a record of Jesus' public ministry, travels, and conflict with Jewish leaders.

Matthew and Luke appear to follow the *encomium* form more closely than Mark or John because they begin with birthing stories. In providing a kingly genealogy up front, Matthew actually starts before Jesus' birth describing Jesus as a son of David and a son of Abraham (Matt 1). Luke dials back to his genealogy after the birthing narrative, but works backward from Jesus to Adam (Luke 3). Mark and John skip the birthing narrative and begin their Gospels with Jesus' baptism and ministry, offering no genealogies at all.

∞

Blessed Lord Jesus,

All praise and honor, power and dominion, truth and justice are yours, because you come to us in the person of Jesus, bone of our bones, flesh of our flesh, a three-dimensional image of God as a living, human being.

Forgive our indifference, our self-absorption, our narcissism in the face of miracle after miracle and blessing after blessing. Turn our attention to you alone.

Thank you for the person of Jesus, who lived a holy, sacrificial life that we might be forgiven and saved from our own obsessions.

In the power of your Holy Spirit, help us to look up at the Father's creation and adore you for what you have done for us.

In the name of the Father, the Son, and the Holy Spirit, Amen.

∞

Questions
1. What was Jesus' given name? Why do we care?
2. What does the atonement mean to you?
3. What literary form is a Gospel?
4. How would you describe the relationship among the Gospels?

Hebrews

> *For since the message declared by angels*
> *proved to be reliable,*
> *and every transgression or disobedience*
> *received a just retribution,*
> *how shall we escape [perdition]*
> *if we neglect such a great salvation?*
> (Heb 2:2–3)

The strongest statement of Christology, the theology of the person, nature, and role of Christ, in the New Testament is found in the Book of Hebrews. A focus on Christology makes sense because the new covenant in Christ is a person (Heb 7:22–24), not a treaty or a set of rules and regulations.

Human and divine, this representative person—"the radiance of the glory of God and the exact imprint of his nature" (Heb 1:3)—is an ideal for Christians to emulate in all aspects of life and ministry. It is accordingly important to understand what makes Jesus unique—his family, his upbringing, his habits, how he thinks, and what he feels. On Christmas, we celebrate the birth of a child—a time in life when a person is most vulnerable, in total need of care and protection.

The subtext in the nativity scene is that Jesus is one of us—complete with dirty diapers. Jesus entered the world in the usual way. His vulnerability being the product of an unwanted pregnancy underscores his humble origins. Being from a small village, not an urban center, gives him street credibility among ordinary people. Being an ethnic Jew means that he is likely mixed race (Num 12:1) because Israel stands between continents—a land disputed among empires as long as there have been any. Jesus' language abilities are unrecorded, although he was likely fluent in Aramaic, Hebrew, and Greek based on various New Testament citations. In America today, Jesus might appear most like a brown-eyed, kinky-haired, Pentecostal pastor from Central America who works in construction during the week and has the physique to prove it.

Origins of the Book of Hebrews

The Book of Hebrews is a sermon likely written in the mid-60s AD written for what was probably a Jewish house church in the city of Rome. The author is unknown, but Martin Luther believed the author to have been Apollo, an educated Jew from Alexandria (Acts 18:24–28) who worked closely with the Apostle Paul. Others, such as Calvin, believed the author to have been Paul (Calvin 2007, 3).

The Book of Hebrews argues the superiority of

Christ to angels, Moses, Aaron, and the prophets, which is an argument that appeals to biblical Jews. It exhorts its audience to remain true to the faith in the face of persecution (Guthrie 1998, 13–35). Hebrews cautions that many followed Moses out of Egypt, but few followed Joshua into the Promised Land (Heb 3:16–19). For Christians, Jesus is the new Joshua who leads us out of sin and into the heavenly kingdom (Murray 1996, 157–158).

Great High Priest

A key verse in the Book of Hebrews is: "For we do not have a high priest who is unable to sympathize with our weaknesses, but one who in every respect has been tempted as we are, yet without sin." (Heb 4:15) A priest serves as an intermediary between God and human beings.

If the priest were merely divine, then the priest, not having any weakness, could not sympathize with mere human beings. If that priest were then also a judge, the judgments would likely be harsh, untempered with an understanding of the limitations and temptations that human beings face.

If the priest were merely human, then how could

the priest have standing with God because God is immortal. The priest could only relate to God during a mortal life being a creature created by God himself—at best a plaything in the hands of immortal God.

Thus, the author of Hebrews argues that the divine and human attributes coexisting in a holy person makes Christ Jesus a suitable candidate to be a great high priest, someone fitting, just, and available. The Book of Hebrews therefore serves to grant us a better understanding of the role and provisions of our great high priest.

∞

Almighty Father,

All praise and honor, power and dominion, truth and justice are yours because you have given us a great high priest in the person of Jesus to mediate for us and with us when we are not in the room.

We confess that our vision is stymied and our hearing imperfect because we refuse to recognize the truth and are unwilling to listen to reason. Forgive us our limited vision and stopped-up ears.

We thank you for the gift of your Son, our savior, Jesus Christ who came to us in the usual way and lived among us despite our unfashionable dress and sinful behavior.

In the power of your Holy Spirit, incite in us a love for you and your church, in season and out, that we might grow closer to you each and every day.

In Jesus' precious name, Amen.

∞

Questions
1. What is Christology?
2. What is the role of a priest, and why do we care?
3. What genre is the Book of Hebrews ,and who wrote it?
4. What is the new covenant?

THE TRANSCENDENCE CHALLENGE

Self-Awareness

> *Now out of the ground the LORD God had formed every beast of the field and every bird of the heavens and brought them to the man to see what he would call them. And whatever the man called every living creature, that was its name.*
> (Gen 2:19)

Transcendence is a basic human quality that has recently come under attack. Transcendence starts, not with our understanding of God, but our understanding of ourselves. Self-awareness is the ability to distinguish the self from surroundings, starting with our mothers and extending to our fathers, siblings, and everyone else. As a father myself, I was always happy to hold my kids, but found it off-putting when they grew old enough to recognize that I was not their mother and would look at mom and cry when I held them. Imagine how God, our Father, must feel when we squirm in his presence and focus on other things.

Confusing the Self

The human mind naturally transcends the body. The human being is one of the few animals that, when confronted with their own image in a mirror, recognizes that the image is of themselves. A healthy self-image is necessary for normal relationships and well-defined boundaries with others and with God. An important problem arises when the boundary between the self and others is fuzzed, or the self is extended to include others, God, or other things.

The attack on transcendence is often motivated by what comes next. After self-awareness, the question arises as how we will relate to the things not contained in the self. For the deconstructionist working hard to deconstruct all power structures, the power of the self to distinguish itself from others raises suspicion because it is potentially the beginning of hegemony. The deconstructionist is more comfortable with unnatural co-dependencies and narcissism where hegemony is harder because the boundary between the self and others is fuzzed. By refusing to recognize legitimate sources of authority, such as God, and undermining the authority of the family, church, and society, deconstructionism furthermore offers no hope to those afflicted by its influence—traditionally the hallmark of demonic influence.

The case of the narcissist is one example of a boundary-management problem between self and others.[1] It ei-

---
[1] A healthy boundary between self and others is like a well-marked property line in real estate (Cloud and Townsend 1992, 25).

ther projects the self onto others, inanimate objects, or animal companions. Or alternatively, rejects any image other than the self. Robert Graves (1972, 115) gives this account of the myth of Narcissus:

> The Goddess Aphrodite [goddess of love] punished Narcissus for being so obstinate [refusing the love of women]. She let him see his own reflection in a pool, as he lay down on the verge to drink, and fall violently in love with it. Whenever he tried to kiss himself, he only got his face wet and spoilt the reflection. Yet he could not bear to leave the pool. At last, in grief and disappointment, he killed himself.

The story of Narcissus is an example of someone who loved the wrong things. If we cannot distinguish self from others, the prospect of a normal love life is nipped in the bud.

Healthy spiritual boundaries begin with distinguishing the self from others and classifying the others as not-self. In the creation account, God makes a number of separations: "And God said, Let there be light, and there was light. And God saw that the light was good. And God separated the light from the darkness." (Gen 1:3–4) Creating light and declaring it to be good and separating it from darkness begins the process of establishing boundaries—

distinguishing the self from other things. Adam's naming of the animals continues this process (Gen 2:19). When God creates Eve and introduces her to Adam, Adam neither confuses her with himself nor with animals. Instead, he falls in love (Gen 2:23).

The Autonomous Self

Why the excursion into psychology? Three reasons stand out. First, an autonomous self is a prerequisite and a product of faith. It is a prerequisite because a person cannot give themselves away to a spouse or to God if they are not in control of themselves. The chains of Satan—addiction, trauma, abuse, fear, fascination with power or the occult, co-dependency, and other psychiatric illnesses—all work to undermine the autonomous self and limit self-control.

Second, an autonomous self is a requirement for freedom in a larger context. Democracy requires that voters make up their own minds independently of one another. If they do not, then an election is nothing more than a census of interest groups. The same logic applies to demand theory in economics. Unless consumers operate independently of one another, competition is undermined and prices are indeterminant. Addiction likewise works to undermine the autonomy of the mind over the body rendering one a slave to an addictive substance. Being created in God's image implies that we are separate from him, not an extension of him.

Third, an autonomous self is a product of faith in the sense that autonomy is always aspirational. Listen to the words of the skeptical father of an epileptic son requesting that Jesus heal him:

> And Jesus said to him, If you can! All things are possible for one who believes. Immediately the father of the child cried out and said, I believe; help my unbelief! (Mark 9:23–24)

If faith were easy, we would all have perfect faith, but none of us do. The journey of faith begins with acknowledging that our own knowledge is limited.

Attacks on the Autonomous Self

The creation account includes one of the first attacks on the autonomous self. In speaking with Eve, Satan twists God's words and attempts to create doubt in Eve's mind: "He said to the woman, "Did God actually say, You shall not eat of any tree in the garden?" (Gen 3:1) By creating doubt in her mind, Satan is acting like the first deconstructionist to undermine God's authority and Eve's faith in God's goodness. Doubt and confusion undermine autonomy by engendering fear and uncertainty, and with it, a heightened propensity to sin under the guise of a false autonomy.

Eve does not sin on her own but only under the influence of Satan. Satan tempts her with false autonomy, leading her to believe that she is autonomous when she, in fact, traded a loving God for Satan, who hates human beings and glories in their destruction. As Jesus says: "The thief [Satan] comes only to steal and kill and destroy." (John 10:10) Only a good and loving God offers his children the security to make real choices and live under his protection.

Sin's attractiveness is why Christ—the son of God—needed to die on the cross to redeem us from sin and Satan's pernicious control. The curse of death imposed by God for sin is a divine curse. Only a divine sacrifice can undo such a divine curse.

∞

Almighty and Merciful Father,

All praise and honor, power and dominion, truth and justice are yours, because you engender our maturity and encourage our autonomy within the context of your love and protection.

Forgive us when we question legitimate sources of authority and power within our daily lives, not caring for the chaos that may result. Be ever near.

Thank you for the gifts of creation and salvation in Christ that we might live in the majesty of the universe that you created and come to you confident of your goodness and love. Guide us in all we feel, think, and do.

In the power of your Holy Spirit, demolish all strongholds of evil in our world, be they malevolent people, structures, or philosophies (2 Cor 10:3–6). Protect our families, churches, and communities.

In Jesus' precious name, Amen.

∞

Questions
1. In what sense is self-awareness an attribute of transcendence?
2. Why is the autonomous self important in faith?
3. What happens when the boundary between self and others is fuzzed?
4. Why is deconstructionism a demonic philosophy?

The Self-Referencing Problem

In the beginning, God created the heavens and the earth.
(Gen 1:1)

A key principle in ontology, the study of existence or being, starts with the realization that everyone has a religion. Religion structures how things knowable and unknowable come together. It is like the machine-language that sits under the operating system on a computer. Refusing structure is like building a house on sand without a foundation (Matt 7:24-27). Ignoring structure carries the price of increasing anxiety and can lead to an existential crisis—a self-implosion—because uncertainty and risk pose problems that cannot be ignored.

The Self-Referencing Problem

At the heart of the existential crisis is a mathematic principle known as Gödel's *Incompleteness Theorem* (1931). Kurt Gödel, a Czech mathematician, was born in 1906, educated in Vienna, and taught at Princeton University. His theorem states that stability in any closed, logical system requires that at least one assumption be taken from outside that system. If creation is a closed, logical system (as having only one set of physical laws suggests that it is) and exhibits stability, then it too must contain at least one external assumption (Smith 2001, 89). This is why computers cannot program themselves and why depressed people are advised to get out of the house and do something outside their normal routine. The stability of the universe depends on the assumption that God exists because he created it.

The Incompleteness Theorem is a system requirement for stability. A system that only references itself is inherently unstable. Any perturbation (disturbance) of the system renders the system dynamically unstable, which is a self-referencing problem. Any reference outside the system offers stability to the entire system, but not all references are equally good.

An example of Gödel's Incompleteness Theorem can be taken from economics. International trade provides an external reference point that stabilizes prices within a particular country's economy. When international trade becomes unstable, this instability is immediately transmitted within the country's price structure. The same effect is present when a bank fails. The financial status of depositors is immediately undermined and panic ensues. This is why banking regulators are quick to intervene and provide liquidity. The self-referencing problem leads to a system that is inherently unstable when change occurs.

Religion Not Optional

Gödel's Incompleteness Theorem suggests why religion is not optional. Religion is an interpretive lens that is foundational to everything that we think or feel. Claiming no religion is not an ontological option unless one is willing to accept anxiety, depression, and/or medication. The frequent assertion that religion is a preference, not a requirement, is an ill-informed position.

A better position is to consider one's options. If one has a problem with Christianity, then what options are available to replace it? Claiming none is to put one ontologically at risk of self-implosion—an existential crisis—which is why narcissists are at high risk of suicide. A substitute should be a better option, not one that places one at risk.

Augustine's Confessions

One person who considered the options was Augustine of Hippo (354–430 AD), whose confessions pictured God as interested in the well-being of individuals. Some believe his confessions began Western Civilization.

Augustine came to faith at the age of thirty-two having struggled with sexual sin. He gave up his career as a teacher of rhetoric and his betrothal to a younger woman so that he could be ordained as a priest. His conversion to Christianity is remarkable, not only because of the things that he gave up, but also because he actively considered the Manichean philosophy and because of the active influence of his Catholic mother, Monica.

Augustine's struggle with sexual passions caused him great anguish before his conversion. The story of the conversion of Victorinus, a fellow professor of rhetoric in Rome, weighed heavily on him. Augustine writes:

> Now when this man of Yours, Simplicianus had told me the story of Victorinus, I was on fire to imitate him: which indeed was why he had told me. He added that in the time of the Emperor Julian, when a law was made prohibiting Christians from teaching Literature and Rhetoric, Victorinus had obeyed the law, preferring to give up his own school of words rather than Your word, by which You make eloquent the tongues of babes. (Foley 2006, 142, 147)

These are not the words of a stoic philosopher. Augustine writes like a man in chains to sin saying: "Thus I was sick at heart and in torment, accusing myself with new intensity of bitterness, twisting and turning in my chain in the hope that it might be utterly broken, for what held me was so small a thing." (Foley 2006, 167).

Augustine wrote this account of his conversion:

> Such things I said, weeping in the most bitter sorrow of my heart. And suddenly I hear a voice from some nearby house, a boy's voice or a girl's voice, I do not know, but it was a sort of sing-song, repeated again and again, 'Take and read, take and read.' (Foley 2006, 169)

Augustine borrowed a book of scriptures from his friend, Alypius, and opened it randomly coming to this verse: "Let us walk properly as in the daytime, not in orgies and drunkenness, not in sexual immorality and sensuality, not in quarreling and jealousy." (Rom 13:13) Convicted of his sexual sin, he took this passage as a word from God to him personally and went to his mother to announce that he was a Christian (Foley 2006, 160).

Augustine's biographer Peter Brown (2000, 157) writes:

> The Confessions…is not a book of reminiscences. They are an anxious turning to the past. The note of urgency is unmistakable. [Augustine writes} Allow me, I beseech You, grant me to wind round and round in my present memory the spirals of my errors…It is also a poignant book. In it, one constantly senses the tension between the 'then' of the young man and the 'now' of the bishop.

Augustine's influence on the church has been enormous. He not only started one of the first monasteries, Martin Luther, an Augustinian monk, helped start the Protestant Reformation about a thousand years later.

∞

Most Merciful Father,

All praise and honor, power and dominion, truth and justice are yours because you care for us personally and lead us step-by-step where you want us to journey.

Forgive the sins of our youth, when we sinned unknowingly and did so even out of spite.

Thank you for your son, our savior, Jesus Christ, who helps us look beyond ourselves to see you and the life that you have in store for us.

In the power of your Holy Spirit, grant us the sense to learn from our mistakes and to grow to learn from other people's mistakes.

In Jesus' precious name, Amen.

∞

Questions
1. What is ontology?
2. What is religion, and why is it not optional?
3. What is Gödel's Incompleteness Theorem? What is the self-referencing problem?
4. Who was Augustine, and why do we care?

Small-T Transcendence

> *In the beginning was the Word,*
> *and the Word was with God,*
> *and the Word was God.*
> (John 1:1)

Virtually any Christology, any theology of Christ, can solve the self-referencing problem—the problem that a closed system requires an external reference to maintain stability. The chief requirement is that the image of Christ be external to the self, not a mirror image of self. The New Testament answer to this problem arose in simply retelling the Jesus story.

The Apostle Paul's writing records several of these early church confessions, for example:

> For I delivered to you as of first importance what I also received: that Christ died for our sins in accordance with the Scriptures, that he was buried, that he was raised on the third day in accordance with the Scriptures, and that he appeared to Cephas [Peter], then to the twelve. (1 Cor 15:3–5)

Much like the citation above from the Apostle John, Jesus is immediately associated with God the Father. More recent attempts to chain Jesus to his humanity suggest a clear departure from the early church norm.

Two Types of Transcendence

The implication of this attempted cleavage between

Jesus, the person, and Jesus, the Son of God, makes it helpful to discuss two types of transcendence. The first type I will call small-T transcendence—any image of Jesus that only solves the self-referencing problem. Any image of Jesus external to the self satisfies the need for an external reference.

Today there are many such images of Jesus that merely satisfy the small-T requirement. Erwin McManus (2021) provides a recent example where he describes Jesus as a religious prodigy. This image of Jesus' humanity renders him palatable to a skeptical generation, but it is like describing Jesus as a prophet or great teacher. It stops short of describing him as divine. Thus, this image of Jesus satisfies only the requirements for small-T transcendence.

The second type I will call large-T transcendence—any image of Jesus that equates him to God the Father, creator of heaven and earth (Gen 1:1). Here Jesus, as the third member of the Trinity, stands outside of time and space because God created both. This is the Jesus of the New Testament who walks on water, heals the sick, exorcizes demons, and rises from the dead.

In the remainder of this reflection, I focus on small-T

transcendence.

The Slippery Slope

Imagine for a moment a mural with sixteen images of Jesus in four rows. In the top lefthand corner is a silhouette of Jesus penned in black. Working across the first row are the same image in brown, green, and yellow colors. In the second row, the silhouette and ordering of colors is reversed. In the third row, the silhouette loses various features of the image and the colors are all shades of grey. In the fourth row, the silhouette morphs step-by-step into an outline of Satan in colors from pink to bright red.

The point of this graphical exercise is to display why the small-T transcendence image of Jesus is dangerous. While the individual is anchored to an external reference, the reference itself is free-floating, not anchored to the story of Jesus given in the New Testament. This is one interpretation of the idolatry problem that we face in postmodern culture.

The Problem of Priorities

Another visual contrast between the God who created heaven and earth, and humanly created idols is found in the Psalms:

> Our God is in the heavens; he does all that he pleases. Their idols are silver and gold, the work of human hands. They have mouths, but do not speak; eyes, but do not see. They have ears, but do not hear; noses, but do not smell. They have hands, but do not feel; feet, but do not walk; and they do not make a sound in their throat. Those who make them become like them; so do all who trust in them. (Ps 115:3–8)

When I read this passage, I am immediately reminded of the bobble-head, plastic Jesuses that sometimes decorates car dashboards. This problem of idolatrous images motivated the writers of the Old Testament to forbid visual images of God (Exod 20:4).

The more insidious images of Jesus are those that we carry around in our heads. While I have focused on the self-reference problem and problem of the free-floating image of Jesus, idolatry can also take the form of false priorities. This happens when we neglect an image of God altogether and make something else our first priority—a person, a job, a philosophy, a political view, a gender, an ethnicity, or a race.

We use our first priority to measure everything else, so it functions differently than other priorities. If my job is my number-one priority, I think of everything in terms of advancement and money. If my spouse is my first priority, then my spouse's opinion is my measure of where I work, what I eat and wear, and to whom I talk. Saying that God is one of our priorities implies that we commit idolatry. If anything other than God is our first priority, we also commit sin, violating the first commandment (Exod 20:3).

∞

Almighty Father,

All praise and honor, power and dominion, truth and justice are yours because you created us and, when we sinned, you offered us a pathway to salvation through Jesus Christ.

Forgive us our wayward hearts, our idolatrous minds, and our treasonous actions. Help us to love the things that you love.

Thank you for the many blessings in this life—our health, our families, our jobs, and our communities. Give us hearts for you alone.

In the power of your Holy Spirit, lift us above the confusion and drama of this life. Lift our eyes to the cross (John 3:14) that we might not stumble or sin.

In the precious name of Jesus, Amen.

∞

Questions
1. What problems can arise with a weak Christology?

Large-T Transcendence

> *Have you not known? Have you not heard?*
> *The LORD is the everlasting God,*
> *the Creator of the ends of the earth.*
> *He does not faint or grow weary; his*
> *understanding is unsearchable.*
> (Isa 40:28)

A popular question floating around today, thanks to the influence of a Hindu sect called Jainism, is how many paths are there up the mountain to God? The presumption in this question is that all religions are equally relevant and subject to personal preferences, nothing more. For the Christian, however, this is a trick question. There are no paths up the mountain to God because God, having created time and space, stands outside of both. We cannot approach God; he must approach us and he did so in the person of Jesus of Nazareth.

Postmodern Context

The spirit of the times refuses to recognize this reality. The prevailing attitude is ABC—Anything But Christian. Postmodernism is radically post-Christian. Much as the Roman Empire was polytheistic, so is postmodern culture. Any religion that claims exclusivity is openly treated with contempt. This contempt is practiced in the media, schools, and every other public forum.

Often people will argue that ABC is just Christian paranoia because public schools sometimes teach from the Bible. The problem is that when people argue that schools teach the Bible, it is to make sure that kids know alternatives to the biblical accounts, such as creation, Noah's flood, and other supernatural events. Before kids have time to develop a faith of their own, they are confronted with alternatives that even their parents cannot sort out. Thus, the multiple-paths-up-the-mountain becomes a focus for teenage rebellion just when secular temptations start to look attractive.

Large-T Transcendence

Before the Big Bang Theory was introduced, creation and science seemed at odds. If you search the Internet for information on the Big Bang Theory (not the television show), the NASA website provides this explanation:

> The big bang is how astronomers explain the way the universe began. It is the idea that the universe began as just a single point, then expanded and stretched to grow as large as it is right now—and it is still stretching!

The theory dates back to 1927 and an astronomer named George Lemaître. This theory gained credibility after another astronomer, Edwin Hubble, observed that other galaxies were moving away from us and the ones farther away were moving away faster.[1]

While people still debate the relationship between the biblical creation accounts and science, the chief thing to know is that the creation accounts focus on the *who* question, not the *how* question that is the focus of science. Genesis states that God created everything (that is, heaven and earth) and then describes a list of things that he has authority over enumerated by days (Niehaus 2014, 39–41). Much as Congress passes laws on a timetable while in session, but the timetable and the implementation need not be tightly linked. If the Big Bang Theory is correct, God can create a surprising number of things in a very short period of time!

The question of transcendence in the case of creation arises because God cannot be part of the created order. A carpenter is not part of the desk that he fashions. This is why God cannot be pictured as a bearded gentleman sitting on top of a mountain. God created both time

---
[1] https://spaceplace.nasa.gov/big-bang/en/#:~:text=The%20Short%20Answer%3A,and%20it%20is%20still%20stretching!

and space, so he must stand apart from both. This is why our entire lives are within his view similar to when one stands on the street in front of an apartment building. One can see all the rooms at once—a perspective not available while standing in any apartment in the building.

Creation Implies Authority

The exclusivity of Christ arises because God created the heavens and the earth. Unlike other creation accounts in the Ancient Near East, God does not contend with monsters to win the universe. Neither does he buy or barter for the universe; neither does he inherit it or find it in a quest. God is sovereign over the universe because he created it.

Because God stands outside time and space, and we do not, we cannot approach God without him coming to us—the very definition of Big-T Transcendence. As Christians, we believe that God sent Jesus Christ to bridge this ontological gap. In the biblical witness, Jesus could be described as Jacob's ladder bridging heaven and earth (Gen 28:12; John 1:51), which is the source of his exclusively. Only someone divine can bridge such a gap. Another gap arises because of God's holiness, which is a restatement of the same ontological gap because holy means set apart as well as sacred. Being set apart in time and space is just one example of the concept of holiness.

God's authority in creation is a problem for anyone conspiring to control other people. Deconstructionists are sensitive on this point because authority denotes power. This is why they challenge every source and manifestation of power as equally illegitimate: Family, church, and society. God's authority is particularly galling for them because it is inherently legitimate and need not be flaunted. Thus, the creation accounts in Genesis are the focus of the deconstructionists efforts to overthrow God's authority.

Implications

God's authority over creation impacts everything we do—past, present, and future. For me, the goodness of God and his love means that I can imitate him and not need to worry about the future. I only need to focus on my faith and relationship with God.

This simplifies everything. Death still stings, but it does not disable. Challenges in work and family life still break my heart, but I am not paralyzed. I am careful to read, understand, and live my Bible, but I do not obsess about prophecies and when God will accomplish them. It is all in the hands of someone powerful whom I trust.

∞

Almighty, Good, and Loving Father,

All praise and honor, power and dominion, truth and justice are yours, because you created and redeemed us that we might call you father.

Forgive us when we forget who we are and who you are. Be ever near.

Thank you for many blessings, but particularly the blessing of a secure future with you.

In the power of your Holy Spirit, lift our eyes and our spirits during this season of winter. Spare us from unnecessary worry that the cold will overwhelm us.

In Jesus' precious name, Amen.

∞

Questions
1. For Christians, how many paths are up the mountain to God?
2. What does ABC mean and why do we care?
3. What does the creation account in Genesis imply about God's sovereignty and authority?
4. Why is it important to distinguish legitimate from illegitimate authority?

Healing Ministry

> *Then Saul said to his servants,*
> *Seek out for me a woman who is a medium,*
> *that I may go to her and inquire of her.*
> *And his servants said to him,*
> *Behold, there is a medium at En-dor.*
> (1 Sam 28:7)

The claim that God has on your life is a direct consequence of his transcendence. It affects life and ministry, and how we respond. Our perception of transcendence follows from our experience of the numinous, the experience of God's presence. Spiritual dreams and visions point beyond themselves to God with scripture as our guide.

The Patient

During my hospital ministry, I was asked to visit with a bedridden, eighty-year-old woman. She was lonely, having been cut off from her family. After several visits, I learned why.

The woman explained that she was frequently visited by her dead mother who advised her not to trust her siblings and she broke off all contact with them. Because she claimed to be a good Baptist, I told her that the Bible forbids speaking with the dead (Lev 19, 20). Entering her world, I advised: "If your mother comes to you again, ask her: What are you doing here? The dead are not supposed to visit with the living." Remember what happened to King Saul (1 Sam 28). After the witch of En-dor conjured up the Prophet Samuel, Samuel prophesied Saul's death.

Reviewing this patient visit, I realized that three responses are typically given to this situation, depending on your worldview:

1. For the materialist lacking any view of transcendence, this woman is hallucinating (a symptom of both Alzheimer's disease and psychosis) and should be referred for psychiatric evaluation (APA 1994, 309).
2. For the Christian limited to small-T transcendence, this woman is in pain and should not have her pain extended through advice—just offer a comforting presence.
3. For the pastor open to large-T transcendence, the woman's pain is less important than the cause of that pain. She was preyed upon by a malevolent spirit dispensing hurtful advice while masquerading as her dead mother.

The malevolent nature of this spirit was obvious from Jesus' teaching: "For no good tree bears bad fruit, nor again does a bad tree bear good fruit, for each tree is known by its own fruit." (Luke 6:43–44)

As shown in this example, the attitude about transcendence directly affects how you approach ministry.

Healing

Jesus was the first medical missionary and his first healing in the Gospel of Mark was an exorcism (Mark 1:23-27). If Jesus is the Son of God and he believes in demons, why do we laugh them off?

Francis MacNutt (2006, 130), who was a priest and is credited with starting the Charismatic Movement within the Catholic Church, spoke about four types of healing: Repentance of sin (spiritual healing), emotional or relational healing, physical healing, and deliverance (healing from spiritual oppression). The transmission of ministry into healing can take many paths, but the most obvious path is through the relief of stress. Stress undermines the body's immune system, leaving one vulnerable to opportunistic diseases (Goleman 2006, 164–185).

Patients whose stress is mitigated will likely experience better physical outcomes, although the healing is nonspecific relative to any particular opportunistic disease. It is common for someone who experienced trauma to develop physical ailments, such as cancer, an infection, or pneumonia during the following year. In my own case, the year after our family was traumatized by a difficult work reorganization and a child born with a life-threatening birth defect, my wife was diagnosed with breast cancer.

Note that my wife's anxiety was external to her person—my job situation, not hers; our son's medical condition, not hers. The anxiety was transmitted through the family system to my wife (e.g. Friedman 1985, 21). Resolution of the anxiety and healing would have needed to deal with the cause, which is not the usual scope for individual counseling. Christians, especially pastors, have the unique advantage of being able to minister to the family system as a whole.

Our Times

The potential for healing today is substantial. During my hospital ministry, I spent a lot of time in the emergency department and noted that about half my patients were there for preventable reasons: Drug treatment, obesity related issues, attempted suicide, and so on. In discussing this observation with the chief surgeon one afternoon, he amended my observation. It's more like three-quarters of the patients. If most of these ailments are preventable, why haven't they been prevented?

At least part of the answer is that the four types of healing articulated by MacNutt simply are being neglected—relievable stress is not being relieved. Because preventable problems, such as declining life expectancy, declining fertility, and declining standards of life, are a theme in our generation, healing ministry should be a priority.

∞

Almighty and Loving Father,

All praise and honor, power and dominion, truth and justice are yours because you see beyond our horizons and have the power to love, heal, and protect in ways that we should emulate. Give us hearts like yours.

Forgive our unwillingness to love, heal, and protect those around us. Give us eyes that see, ears that hear, and hands that heal.

Thank you for the example of Jesus of Nazareth, whose willingness to break through the prejudices and limited vision of his time was followed by his actions. May we grow more like him with each passing day.

In the power of your Holy Spirit, be with us, inspire us, and extend us so that your church may grow to encompass all in need.

In Jesus' precious name, Amen.

∞

Questions
1. In what ways can our view of transcendence widen our field of vision?
2. What extraordinary events have you witnessed? What was your response?
3. What four aspects of healing did Francis MacNutt articulate?
4. What role does stress play in the immune system and healing?

OLD TESTAMENT PROPHECIES

The Mission

The Spirit of the Lord GOD is upon me,
because the LORD has anointed me
to bring good news to the poor;
he has sent me to bind up the brokenhearted,
to proclaim liberty to the captives,
and the opening of the prison to those who are bound;
to proclaim the year of the LORD's favor,
and the day of vengeance of our God;
to comfort all who mourn;
(Isa 61:1–2)

The Gospel of Matthew offers at least three visions of Jesus' mission. The first is theological, encompassed in his name. "You shall call his name Jesus, for he will save his people from their sins." (Matt 1:21) The second is political: "I was sent only to the lost sheep of the house of Israel." (Matt 15:24) The third vision is missional. It references Isaiah 61, which his call sermon cites (Luke 4) and the Beatitudes allude to (Matt 5).

The Atonement

The name Jesus is a Greek translation of Joshua that arises because Greek has no *sh* sound to transliterate the Hebrew.

Joshua's call is informative: "Moses my servant is dead. Now therefore arise, go over this Jordan, you and all this people, into the land that I am giving to them, to the people of Israel." (Josh 1:2) While Joshua led the people of Israel out of the desert into the Promised Land, Jesus leads his people out of bondage to sin into heaven (Murray 1996, 157–158).

The atonement of Christ is a theme in the Servant Songs of the Book of Isaiah. Duane Lindsey (1985, 4) writes: "Jesus summarized his mission by affirming that even the Son of Man did not come to be served, but to serve, and to give his life as a ransom for many" (Mark 10:45). He sees the servant empowered with three tasks: 1. Effecting a new covenant for Israel, 2. Being a light to the nations, and 3. Delivering the spiritually blind (Lindsey 1985, 53, 55, 69). These three tasks would not necessarily appeal to an ethnic Jew because the relationship between God and Israel would no longer be exclusive.

Woman at the Well

Jesus' meeting with the woman at Jacob's well in Sychar (John 4:4–30) was highly symbolic and pointed to the objective of reunifying the Nation of Israel.

First, Sychar is in Samaria, which most Jews avoided. Jews routinely went out of their way to walk around Samaria when traveling north to Galilee from Judea. In order for Jesus to unite the Kingdom of David again, Samaria and Judah must be reconciled. Casting a favorable light on Samaritans also shows up in Jesus' Parable of the Good Samaritan (Luke 10:25–37) and in Jesus' healing of the ten lepers (Luke 17:11–17).

Second, Sychar was where Dinah, daughter of Jacob, was raped by Shechem, the son of Hamor the Hivite (Gen 34:2). Dinah's brothers, Simeon and Levi, tricked Shechem and all the men of his city into being circumcised, presumably to marry Dinah, then killed them all while they convalesced. Because of this evil act (and Reuben's sin in sleeping with one of Jacob's wives, Gen 35:22), Jacob later blessed Judah to lead the family (Gen 49:1–10). King David and Jesus were both of the tribe of Judah.

Jesus' meeting with the woman at the well serves as a mirror image of the story of Dinah. Instead of an unrighteous man raping an innocent woman, a righteous man heals an unrighteous woman. The importance of this symbolic act is perhaps why Jesus revealed his messiahship (John 4:25–26) and the nature of true worship to the woman:

But the hour is coming, and is now here, when

> the true worshipers will worship the Father in spirit and truth, for the Father is seeking such people to worship him. God is spirit, and those who worship him must worship in spirit and truth. (John 4:23–24)

The observation that Jesus' first evangelist is a woman of Samaria implies that reunification of King David's united Kingdom of Israel is an important objective (John 4:29).

Third, King Solomon's son, Rehoboam, planned to be crowned at Shechem, but because of an unwise decision about taxation, the Northern Kingdom revolted under the leadership of Jeroboam (1 Kgs 12:1). Jesus describes his mission as "I was sent only to the lost sheep of the house of Israel." (Matt 15:24) While many viewed Israel as consisting only of Judah, the United Kingdom of Israel under King David and his son, Solomon, consisted of both the Northern Kingdom (ten tribes, also known as Samaria and Israel) and Southern kingdom (the tribes of Judah and Benjamin).

Jeroboam worried that if the people continued traveling to Jerusalem to worship, they would return to King Rehoboam, so he cast two golden calves. He placed one in Bethel and the other in Dan (1 Kgs 12:27–29). This act was later referred to as the Sin of Jeroboam. The Samaritan religion he founded continues to exist today.

In healing the woman at the well, Jesus effectively exorcized two national curses: The rape of Dineh and the division of Israel. For us, these stories appear as a template for pastoral care under the guidance of the Holy Spirit, but for his immediate audience Jesus would have been perceived as uniting the lost sheep of Israel (Matt 15:24).

∞

Beloved Lord Jesus,

All praise and honor, power and dominion, truth and justice are yours because you worked to reunify the nation of Israel and to save us from our sins. Be ever near.

Forgive our myopia—our preoccupation with the minutia of our own private lives and our unwillingness to consider those around us. Be ever near.

Thank you for the gift of your life and ministry among us that we might be reconciled with our families, friends, and neighbors, and reconciled with you. Be ever near.

In the power of your Holy Spirit, teach us to love the things that you love.

In Jesus' precious name, Amen.

Questions
1. What two objectives does the Gospel of Matthew see in Jesus?
2. What is the meaning of Jesus' name?
3. What two events occurred in Sychar that were important in the history of the Nation of Israel?
4. When and why did the Northern and Southern Kingdoms separate?

Messiah Described

> *For to us a child is born, to us a son is given;*
> *and the government shall be upon his shoulder,*
> *and his name shall be called Wonderful Counselor, Mighty*
> *God, Everlasting Father, Prince of Peace.*
> *Of the increase of his government and of peace*
> *there will be no end, on the throne of David*
> *and over his kingdom, to establish it*
> *and to uphold it with justice*
> *and with righteousness from this time forth and forevermore.*
> *The zeal of the LORD of hosts will do this.*
> (Isa 9:6–7)

In the Jewish tradition, a messiah is someone anointed with oil as a priest, prophet, or king. The first reference in the Old Testament to anointing arises with regard to Aaron being anointed priest (Exod 28:41), but in Elijah's swain song, he is instructed to anoint both a king and a prophet: "And Jehu the son of Nimshi you shall anoint to be king over Israel, and Elisha the son of Shaphat of Abel-meholah you shall anoint to be prophet in your place." (1 Kgs 19:16) The term *messiah* is itself used biblically only twice in the Gospel of John where it is immediately translated into the Greek term *Christ* (John 1:41, 4:25).

Descriptions of the Messiah are lengthiest and most frequent in the Book of Isaiah, which is widely quoted during Advent and in Christmas carols and readings. Consider Isaiah 9:6–7 cited above or this description of the

Messiah's origins, described by Pass and Nietert (2023, 250) as the sevenfold spirits of God:

> There shall come forth a shoot from the stump of Jesse, and a branch from his roots shall bear fruit. And the Spirit of the LORD shall rest upon him, the Spirit of wisdom and understanding, the Spirit of counsel and might, the Spirit of knowledge and the fear of the LORD. And his delight shall be in the fear of the LORD. He shall not judge by what his eyes see, or decide disputes by what his ears hear, but with righteousness he shall judge the poor, and decide with equity for the meek of the earth; and he shall strike the earth with the rod of his mouth, and with the breath of his lips he shall kill the wicked. (Isa 11:1–4)

Jesse is the father of King David (1 Sam 16:1). Isaiah writes from 739 BC to 681 BC, which implies that his prophesy of the suffering servant was recorded centuries before the birth of Jesus Christ (Lindsey 1985, 17) during "the days of Uzziah, Jotham, Ahaz, and Hezekiah, kings of Judah." (Isa 1:1) According to tradition, Isaiah died after being sawed in two (Heb 11:37).

Servant Songs

While Isaiah describes the Messiah in many passages, the most famous have to do with his servant songs. Lindsey (1985) outlines four particular passages as these servant songs: The Call (Isa 42:1–9), the Commission (Isa

49:1–13), the Commitment (Isa 50:4–11), and the Career (Isa 52:13–53:12).

In the first servant song, the servant is empowered to effect a new covenant for Israel, be a light to the nations, and deliver the spiritually blind (Lindsey 1985, 53, 55, 69). Lindsey (1985, 35) notes that "Yahweh proves that He controls history by demonstrating his ability to prophesy."

The second servant song reinforces the first but does not forget Israel. Lindsey (1985, 77) writes: "Yahweh's called and gifted Servant is rejected at first by His own people Israel, but in a future day of grace He will ultimately succeed not only in fulfilling an expanded mission to bring salvation to the Gentiles but also in restoring Israel both to the land (physically and politically) and to Yahweh (spiritually)."

The third servant song "amplifies the suffering and patient endurance of the Servant." (Lindsey 1985, 79) Isaiah writes: "I gave my back to those who strike, and my cheeks to those who pull out the beard; I hid not my face from disgrace and spitting." (Isa 50:6)

Lindsey (1985, 97) sees the fourth servant song as the most important text in the Old Testament. A key verse is:

> But he was pierced for our transgressions; he was crushed for our iniquities; upon him was the chastisement that brought us peace, and with his wounds we are healed. (Isa 53:5)

This is a clear statement of the atonement.

Messiah as Redeemer

Few will forget the description of God more generally in Isaiah's call:

> In the year that King Uzziah died I saw the Lord sitting upon a throne, high and lifted up; and the train of his robe filled the temple. (Isa 6:1)

Yet it is the call of the Nation of Israel that I pinned on my office wall during my darkest days:

> But now thus says the LORD, he who created you, O Jacob, he who formed you, O Israel: "Fear not, for I have redeemed you; I have called you by name, you are mine. When you pass through the waters, I will be with you; and through the rivers, they shall not overwhelm you; when you walk through fire you shall not be burned, and the flame shall not consume you. For I am the LORD your God, the Holy One of Israel, your Savior. I give Egypt as your ransom, Cush and Seba in exchange for you. Because you are precious in my eyes, and honored, and I love you, I give men in return for you, peoples in exchange for your life. (Isa 43:1–4)

While this passage summarizes the history of the Nation

of Israel, allegorically it refers to all of God's elect and also defines the role of the Messiah as a redeemer of Israel. Other summaries (e.g. Ps 103, Acts 7) are not nearly so hopeful.

The role of a redeemer is defined in Leviticus 25:23–33. It is extensively cited in the Old Testament, but especiallg in Isaiah,[1] who describes God himself as the redeemer. Isaiah is not alone in picturing God a redeemer. Consider the prayer: "Let the words of my mouth and the meditation of my heart be acceptable in your sight, O LORD, my rock and my redeemer." (Ps 19:14) Or Job 19:25: "For I know that my Redeemer lives, and at the last he will stand upon the earth." (Job 19:25).

While redemption has to do with buying back property that has been sold or captives lost in battle to an enemy, atonement is a legal term that has to do with cleansing from sin: The priest "shall make atonement for the Holy Place, because of the uncleannesses of the people of Israel and because of their transgressions, all their sins." (Lev 16:16) The holiness of the people is—so speak—redeemed

---
[1] Lev 25:25, Ruth 3:9,12, 4:1, 3, 6, 8,14, Job 19:25, Ps 19:14, 78:35, Prov 23:11, Isa 41:14, 43:14, 44:6, 24, 47:4, 48:17, 49:7, 26, 54:5, 8, 59:20, 60:16, 63:16, Jer 50:34, Acts 7:35

through a blood offering. Christ's death on the cross both redeemed us from sin and atoned (or expiated) for that sin. This distinction between redemption and atonement exists in scripture but is lost on us because for Christians the sacrificial system ended with the cross.

∞

Most Merciful Father,

All praise and honor, power and dominion, truth and justice are yours because you redeemed our lives from the pit, atoned for our sin through your death on the cross, and anointed our heads with the oil of salvation (2 Cor 1:21). Be ever near.

Forgive our denial of your divinity, denial of our sinful nature, and denial of your love through a lifetime of wanton mindlessness. Be ever near.

Thank you for making yourself available to us through the ministry of your son and the gift of your Holy Spirit. Be ever near.

In the power of your Holy Spirit, heal our sin sick ways and draw us closer to you with each passing day. Open our hearts, illumine our minds, strengthen our hands in your service.

In Jesus' precious name, Amen.

Questions
1. What is a Messiah?
2. What is the picture of the Messiah given in the book of Isaiah?
3. What is redemption? How does it differ from atonement?
4. Why is atonement an obsolete term for Christians?

New Covenant

> *For this is the covenant that I will make*
> *with the house of Israel after those days,*
> *declares the LORD: I will put my law within them,*
> *and I will write it on their hearts.*
> *And I will be their God, and they shall be my people.*
> (Jer 31:33)

A key prophecy of the Messiah found in the first Servant Song is:

> I am the LORD; I have called you in righteousness; I will take you by the hand and keep you; I will give you as a covenant for the people, a light for the nations, to open the eyes that are blind, to bring out the prisoners from the dungeon, from the prison those who sit in darkness. (Isa 42:6–7)

Note the phrase: "I will give you as a covenant for the people." (Isa 42:6) The Hebrew word here means: "1. alliance of friendship 2. covenant, as a divine constitution or ordinance with signs or pledges."[1] The Greek translation means:

> Generation of a formal arrangement or agreement for disposing of something in a manner assuring continuity, covenant – a. with focus on testamentary aspect last will and testament b. with focus on OT perspective of God's unilaterally assumed obligation to confer a special blessing.[2]

What stands out in the Isaiah passage is that this new cov-

---

[1] berit (בְּרִית DBD 285)
[2] diatheke (διαθήκη BDAG 1847)

enant is not a written document, like the covenant given to Moses (e.g. Exod 20), it is a person. In the Jeremiah passage (Jer 31:33), this new covenant is not written on stone or on parchment, but on human hearts. This new covenant accordingly differs qualitatively from previous covenants, like the covenants with Abraham or with Moses.

Promises and Covenants

Robert Jenson (1973, 2) writes: "A promise poses a future in a very particular way: as a gift." Creation is clearly a gift for Adam and Eve, And, by inference, for us. Jenson (1973, 8) interprets the Gospel as promise and views it as the grammatical anthesis of law.

> Because I will do such and such, you may await such and such. The pattern is 'Because…, therefore…,' the reverse of 'If…, then…' Here the future is opened independent of any prior condition…it grants a future free from the past.

This contrast between a promise, which is unconditional, and a covenant, which has conditions, highlights the difference between law and Gospel, although promises and covenants are also related because we can make promises, especially with God, that may not be consummated with words.

My call to ministry started with a promise at the

foot of a hospital bed. My son was born with only one kidney and that kidney became blocked when he was only ten weeks old. Desperate, I found myself negotiating with God for my son's life: *Don't take him; take me.*

God answered my praryer. My son had a series of successful surgeries. Later, he went through dialysis and a transplant. About ten years later, I realized that God does not want to take lives. He wants for us to dedicate ourselves in life to his ministry. This is when I began to seek a seminary where I might learn what a life devoted to God means.

The Abrahamic Covenant

God's relationship with Abraham began with a promise and instructions:

> Now the LORD said to Abram, Go from your country and your kindred and your father's house to the land that I will show you. And I will make of you a great nation, and I will bless you and make your name great, so that you will be a blessing. I will bless those who bless you, and him who dishonors you I will curse, and in you all the families of the earth shall be blessed. (Gen 12:1–3)

You might describe these instructions as a loyalty test that is also extended to us because Abraham comes to us as a representative person of faith. Learning to depend on God is formative, so Abraham's experience is also a coming-of-age story, even though Abraham was seven-five years old at the time (Gen 12:4).

To confirm this promise, Abraham and God himself engage in a cutting ceremony where a heifer, a ram, a dove, and a pigeon are cut in half. God then appears in a dream to walk between these cut carcasses in the form of "a smoking fire pot and a flaming torch" (Gen 15:9–17). The symbolism is striking and parallels the cutting ceremony between a suzerain (lord of lords) and his vassals. The idea here is that the covenant between the overlord and his vassals is sealed in blood, where the vassal promises to keep the covenant or end up like the slaughtered animals. This is why a blood sacrifice is required to atone for sin. Sin is an act of rebellion and breaks the covenant, triggering the stipulation.

God later uses explicit covenantal language to refer to this same promise with Abraham: "This is my covenant, which you shall keep, between me and you and your offspring after you: Every male among you shall be circumcised." (Gen 17:10) Abram is renamed Abraham in this account (Gen 17:5). Note the cutting involved in circumcision and the first act of marriage. The form of the covenants found in Genesis follow the form of "Second Millennium BC Hittite suzerain-vassal treaties" (Niehaus 2014, 37), which is important in understanding the context and dating of the text.

The Covenant With Moses

As Christians, we are more familiar with the Mosaic covenant that has been written down. The Abrahamic covenant, while long on ceremony, is short on stipulations, unlike the Mosaic covenant that not only includes the Ten Commandments, but also lengthy case law enumerated in the Book of Leviticus. This makes the Abrahamic covenant more relational than the Mosaic covenant. This difference suggests a potential problem—one could presumably obey the Mosaic covenant and neglect transcendence, having no relationship with God.

Returning to Relationship

Jesus' interpretation of the Mosaic law suggests this tension between relationship and law-keeping is the core problem being addressed in the new covenant that was to be written on our hearts.

Consider Jesus' segment in the Sermon on the Mount initiated with the repeated phrase: "You have heard that it was said" (Matt 5:21, 27, 33, 38, and 43). This segment begins an interpretation of the stipulations of the Mosaic covenant covering murder, adultery, and false witness. It goes on to interpret revenge and love of neighbor. In each case, the Pharisees have narrowly defined the stipulations so that they could be obeyed, while Jesus widened the stipulations to talk about the attitudes leading to disobedience.

In the case of murder, we read:

> You have heard that it was said to those of old, You shall not murder; and whoever murders will be liable to judgment. But I say to you that everyone who is angry with his brother will be liable to judgment; whoever insults his brother will be liable to the council; and whoever says, You fool! will be liable to the hell of fire. (Matt 5:21–22)

By including anger in the prohibition of murder, Jesus makes law-keeping impossible without the guidance of the Holy Spirit. The law is therefore fulfilled in developing our relationship with God. In effect, we grow closer to God in keeping the commandments.

As Christians we recognize this as the role of the

Holy Spirit. The law is fulfilled in developing our relationship with God through the Holy Spirit. It allows us both to grow closer to God and to keep the commandments.

∞

Almighty Father,

All praise and honor, power and dominion, truth and justice are yours, because you commit yourself and bind us to yourself in covenants and promises.

Be patient with our wandering hearts. Forgive our wayward ways. Teach us to love one another and love you more fully.

Thank you for the scriptures that remind us of your relationship with our ancestors, parents, and loved ones.

In the power of your Holy Spirit, draw us to yourself. Open our hearts; illumine our minds; strengthen our hands in your service.

In Jesus' precious name, Amen.

∞

Questions
1. What is a covenant?
2. Why do we use the phrase: Cut a covenant?
3. How does the Abrahamic covenant differ from the Mosaic covenant?
4. What problem does Jesus highlight with the Mosaic covenant?

The Story of Isaac

> *By faith Abraham, when he was tested, offered up Isaac, and he who had received the promises was in the act of offering up his only son, of whom it was said, Through Isaac shall your offspring be named.*
> (Heb 11:17–18)

Few references in the Old Testament are as important in Christology as the story of Isaac. When God promised Abraham "I will make of you a great nation" (Gen 12:2) and "To your offspring I will give this land" (Gen 12:7), Abraham was already seventy-five years old (Gen 12:4). Furthermore, Abraham's wife, Sarai, was both past child-bearing age and barren (Gen 11:30), even if she was beautiful in her old age (Gen 12:11). This unfulfilled promise tested Abraham's faith.

The Hagar Incident

The Hagar incident simply confirmed that no one believed that Sarai could have children, least of all Sarai herself (Gen 16:1–8). In the ancient world, infertility could be handled through offering your husband a slave woman, which Sarai did (Gen 16:2). When Hagar became pregnant, Sarai became jealous and treated her so badly that Hagar ran away. The Lord appeared to Hagar in the desert and told her to return to her mistress and gave her a prophecy of Ishmael (Gen 16:4–12). So Hagar returned to her mistress.

Abraham was eighty-six years old when Hagar bore him a son, Ishmael (Gen 16:16).

The Promise Reiterated

Yet, God's promise to Abraham was through Sarai:

> And God said to Abraham, As for Sarai your wife, you shall not call her name Sarai, but Sarah shall be her name. I will bless her, and moreover, I will give you a son by her. I will bless her, and she shall become nations; kings of peoples shall come from her. (Gen 17:15–16)

Isaac means "he laughed" in Hebrew for a reason. Neither Abraham nor Sarah believed that they could have a child and both laughed when they were told. At the time of this promise to Sarai, Abraham was one hundred years old and Sarai was ninety (Gen 17:17). When Isaac was born nine month's later, he was a miracle baby.

Inheritance Squabble

A child born to a slave, such as Hagar, would legally belong to the infertile wife and would have the same inheritance rights as a child born to the wife. After Sarah had Isaac, she realized that Ishmael was Abraham's first-born son and would receive the majority of the inheritance.

Jealous for her son, she had Abraham free Hagar and send her away (Gen 21:9–10), which was cruel but within her legal rights.

The story of Hagar's prayer and God's rescue (Gen 21:11–21) is particularly significant for Muslims, who claim Ishmael as their ancestor. Ishmael's genealogy is recorded in Genesis 25:12–18.

Hagar Symbolizes Law

The Apostle Paul took the story of Hagar and Sarah allegorically to represent the old and new covenants (Gal 4:23–26). This allegory comparing Hagar with law and Sarah with Gospel makes the point that our relationship with God is not something forced or codified, but alive and freely given in Jesus Christ.

Mount Moriah

The incident at Mount Moriah started with a command from God:

> After these things God tested Abraham and said to him, Abraham! And he said, Here I am. He said, Take your son, your only son Isaac, whom you love, and go to the land of Moriah, and offer him there as a burnt offering on one of the mountains of which I shall tell you. (Gen 22:1–2)

The idea of a child sacrifice to a god was well-attested in

the Ancient Near East and only abolished in the Roman Empire in 97 AD.[1] While often veiled beneath the religious ceremony, like worship of Baal or Asherah (Jer 19:4–6), child sacrifice, much like abortion today, was typically motivated by economic problems, like poverty, crop failure, and starvation, and it was more likely to involve female babies. In the case of Isaac, this sacrifice is proposed as a loyalty test for Abraham and stands out because a male child is involved.[2]

The text describes Isaac as a boy or young man, even though the story of Hagar almost immediately precedes this one, which is reinforced by comment that Isaac carried the wood for the sacrifice (Gen 22:5–6). Some commentators make the point that Abraham, as an old man, could not chase down a teenage boy and bind him, if he were to resist. This suggests that Isaac was a willing participant in the sacrifice.

Having bound Isaac and laid him on the altar, the story goes on:

---

[1] https://en.wikipedia.org/wiki/Human_sacrifice.
[2] A modern example is the response to the one-child policy in China adopted in 1979. The availability of abortion led to significantly more (circa 20 percent more) male babies being carried to term than female babies, and a dramatic population imbalance (Kirkpatrick 2012, 78–81).

> Then Abraham reached out his hand and took the knife to slaughter his son. But the angel of the LORD called to him from heaven and said, Abraham, Abraham! And he said, Here I am. He said, Do not lay your hand on the boy or do anything to him, for now I know that you fear God, seeing you have not withheld your son, your only son, from me. (Gen 22:10–12)

Abraham passed the loyalty test and God reiterates his promise to Abraham that he would become the father of many nations (Gen 22:15–17).

Abraham's willingness to sacrifice Isaac on Mount Moriah is an allegory to Jesus' death on the cross. Because Abraham did not withhold his son, neither did God[3] (Heb 11:17–19; Jam 2:21).

∞

Almighty Father,

All praise and honor, power and dominion, truth and justice are yours, because you did not withhold your son, but offered him as a sacrifice on the cross that we might be forgiven.

We confess that we are not worthy to be called your sons and daughters. We can only approach you as your children because of the blood of Jesus.

---

[3] The Temple Mount in Jerusalem is believed by some to be the site of Mount Moriah. Muslims believe that Ishmael, not Isaac, was the intended sacrifice.

Thank you for your mercy. Let us never forget.

In the power of your Holy Spirit, draw us to yourself. Open our hearts, illumine our thoughts, strengthen our hands in your service.

In Jesus' precious name, Amen.

∞

Questions
1. What was special about Isaac?
2. Who was Ishmael?
3. What happened on Mount Moriah?
4. Why did Sarah send Hagar away?

Christ Figures

> *I will put enmity between you and the woman,*
> *and between your offspring and her offspring;*
> *he shall bruise your head, and you shall bruise his heel.*
> (Gen 3:15)

The term, Christ figure, is an informal, literary reference to deliverer, redeemer, or messiah found even in popular literature (e.g. Schaefer 2013). The focus is on the external struggle:

> And when all these things come upon you, the blessing and the curse, which I have set before you, and you call them to mind among all the nations where the LORD your God has driven you, and return to the LORD your God, you and your children, and obey his voice in all that I command you today, with all your heart and with all your soul, then the LORD your God will restore your fortunes and have mercy on you, and he will gather you again from all the peoples where the LORD your God has scattered you. (Deut 30:1–3)

Walter Brueggemann (2016, 59) describes this passage as the Deuteronomic Cycle, which he paraphrases as collective sin, scattering, enslavement, crying out to the Lord, and the sending of a deliverer. The suffering of Christ figures in the Old Testament experience could be as much internal as external.

Joseph as a Christ Figure

This deliverance is often embodied in charismatic

leadership. The first hint of this deliverer in Genesis 3, cited at the beginning of this section, shows up in spiritual warfare—a clash of the divine and the demonic.

In the Joseph story, this spiritual conflict is primarily internal. Born to Jacob's favorite wife, Rachel, Joseph is sold into slavery in Egypt by his jealous brothers (Gen 30:24, 37:28). Joseph is talented, faithful, and gifted by God with the ability to interpret dreams, but he must learn to channel his gifts with sensitivity. Joseph must also overcome his own self-pity and hatred of his brothers before he can deliver his family from drought and starvation.

Joseph overcomes his internal struggle and becomes a deliverer of his people once he learns to forgive his brothers: "As for you, you meant evil against me, but God meant it for good, to bring it about that many people should be kept alive, as they are today." (Gen 50:20) As a Christ figure, Joseph is interesting because we normally interpret spiritual warfare as an external struggle, not an internal one.

Moses as a Christ Figure

The archetype of this external struggle shows up in Moses' confrontation with Pharaoh:

> So Moses and Aaron went to Pharaoh and did just as the LORD commanded. Aaron cast down his staff before Pharaoh and his servants, and it became a serpent. Then Pharaoh summoned the wise men and the sorcerers, and they, the magicians of Egypt, also did the same by their secret arts. For each man cast down his staff, and they became serpents. But Aaron's staff swallowed up their staffs. (Exod 7:9–12)

God himself mediates this confrontation between Moses and Pharaoh. He instructs Moses as to what he should do, which models our dependence on the Holy Spirit in such power encounters. Still, Moses might be described as an Old Testament Christ figure because with God's mediation he delivers the Nation of Israel from the hand of Pharaoh, symbolized in this passage by Aaron's staff swallowing the staves of the Egyptian sorcerers and magicians.

We often gloss over Moses' backstory and internal struggle, but Moses could not return to Egypt until he overcame his fear. Moses had murdered an Egyptian and was exiled for forty years in the deserts of Midian. Thus, the deliverance of Israel from the Egyptians started with Moses' struggle to deal with his fear of being prosecuted for murdering an Egyptian (Exod 2:11–15).

Gideon as Christ Figure

The Book of Judges repeats the Deuteronomic cycle introducing many examples of charismatic leadership. One popular example of charismatic leadership is Gideon.

Gideon'sstory begins: "The people of Israel did what was evil in the sight of the LORD, and the LORD gave them into the hand of Midian seven years." (Jdg 6:1) The people of Israel call out to God (Jdg 6:6), and God sends an angel to Gideon to call him into leadership. With only three hundred men, Gideon then defeats the army of the Midianites (Jdg 7:25).

Again, while we often remember Gideon's victory over the Midianites, his own struggle with fear initially holds him back. Listen to Gideon's prayer:

> And he said to him, Please, Lord, how can I save Israel? Behold, my clan is the weakest in Manasseh, and I am the least in my father's house. And the LORD said to him, But I will be with you, and you shall strike the Midianites as one man. (Jdg 6:15–16)

Gideon's faith is also weak. Consider one of several tests that God gives him:

> That night the LORD said to him, Take your father's bull, and the second bull seven years old, and pull down the altar of Baal that your father has, and cut down the Asherah that is beside it and build an altar to the LORD your God on the top of the stronghold here, with stones laid in due order. Then take the second bull and offer it as a

> burnt offering with the wood of the Asherah that you shall cut down. So Gideon took ten men of his servants and did as the LORD had told him. But because he was too afraid of his family and the men of the town to do it by day, he did it by night. (Jdg 6:25–27)

Through a series of such tests, Gideon's faith grows and with it comes support from the wider community of Israel.

These Christ figures in the Old Testament anticipate the coming of Christ in the New Testament. They also show how internal faith challenges must be overcome in growing into leadership, which we might as Christians recognize as the role of the Holy Spirit in our own lives.

∞

Almighty Father,

All praise and honor, power and dominion, truth and justice are yours, because you have given us Christ figures to aid in overcoming our own weaknesses and fear. Help us to do better.

Forgive our unwillingness to pay attention to your scriptures and the leanings of the Holy Spirit. Help us to do better.

Thank you for the examples of Moses, Joseph, and Gideon. Help us to learn from their examples.

In the power of your Holy Spirit, grant us the willingness and ability to deal with our weaknesses and to confront our fears that we might become leaders in your church.

> In Jesus' precious name, Amen.

∞

Questions
1. What is a Christ figure? Why is the Deuteronomic Cycle helpful in understanding them?
2. What is the first example of spiritual warfare in the Bible?
3. What were Joseph's issues? How about Moses? Gideon?
4. How does the Holy Spirit figure into developing our full potential as Christians?

THE APOSTLE PAUL

Paul's Conversion

> *Now as he went on his way, he approached Damascus, and suddenly a light from heaven shone around him. And falling to the ground, he heard a voice saying to him, Saul, Saul, why are you persecuting me? And he said, Who are you, Lord? And he said, I am Jesus, whom you are persecuting.*
> (Acts 9:3–5)

If the Apostle Paul wrote first and set the tone for the New Testament, then his faith story is critically important. Before his conversion, Paul was primarily known by his Hebrew name, Saul. (Acts 13:9).

Paul's Conversion

No one anticipated Paul's conversion, least of all Paul. Paul traveled to Damascus to arrest Christians and stamp out the church. The text makes it clear that he was obsessed with his mission of persecuting the church (Acts 9:1-2). As cited above, Paul's plans changed when he encountered the Risen Christ.

Paul's conversion experience on the road to Damascus is repeated three times in the Book of Acts (Acts 9:1–20, 22:4–21, 26:9–23). The first telling is simply part of the narration by the writer of the Book of Acts. The second is a speech given during a riot in the Temple in Jerusalem. The third is a presentation in Caesarea before King Agrippa.

In each case the dialogue contains the same words given above, but in the third case Jesus also says enigmatically: "It is hard for you to kick against the goads." (Acts 26:14) A goad is a spiked stick used to guide a pack animal.

We are not told what goads Paul kicked against, but we might infer from the context that he ignored the testimony of the Christians that he had arrested—a sort of spiritual deafness—until he met Jesus on the road to Damascus.

Paul's Mission

Paul's mission is also given in each of the three accounts. In the first account, the mission is given in a vision to Ananias:

> But the Lord said to him [Ananias], Go, for he is a chosen instrument of mine to carry my name before the Gentiles and kings and the children of Israel. For I will show him how much he must suffer for the sake of my name. (Acts 9:15–16)

In the second account, Jesus tells him: "Rise, and go into Damascus, and there you will be told all that is appointed for you to do." (Acts 22:10) Later, Jesus gives him details in a trance (Acts 22:17). In the third account, Jesus tells him:

> But rise and stand upon your feet, for I have appeared to you for this purpose, to appoint you as

> a servant and witness to the things in which you have seen me and to those in which I will appear to you, delivering you from your people and from the Gentiles—to whom I am sending you to open their eyes, so that they may turn from darkness to light and from the power of Satan to God, that they may receive forgiveness of sins and a place among those who are sanctified by faith in me. (Acts 26:16–18)

In this third account, we hear an echo of the call of the Prophet Ezekiel (2:1). At this point Paul is paying attention to the visions of his peers, such as Ananias, and his own visions, indicates spiritual attentiveness and growth. This is big step up from kicking against the goads.

Paul's encounter with the Risen Christ has clearly been a catalyst for spiritual growth.

Separation From Judaism

E.P. Sanders (1977, 552) in his exhaustive study of what distinguishes the Apostle Paul's writing from other Jews in the first century writes:

> In saying that participationist eschatology is different from covenantal nomism, I mean only to say that it differs, not that the difference is instructive for seeing the error of Judaism's way.

By participationist eschatology, Sanders is referring to passages like "For if we have been united with him in a death like his, we shall certainly be united with him in a resurrection like his." (Rom 6:5) The Greek word translated here as united[1] is unique to Paul and used nowhere else in the New Testament. It expresses this idea of participation that Sanders focuses on.

In other words, we should emulate Jesus' life story in order to participate in his glory now and in the future (also Phil 3:10–11). This salvation arises, not in adhering to the laws given in the Mosaic covenant (e.g. covenantal nomism), but in living in Christ, which is Paul's expression for modeling our lives after Jesus' example. Sanders sees this break with Judaism as coming not so much from Paul's conversion story or the political break with Judaism in the rebellion against Rome, but in the substance of Paul's theology. God's new covenant arises in following Christ's example.

Paul writes explicitly about this break in his own life, which is often glossed over:

> Therefore, O King Agrippa, I was not disobedient to the heavenly vision, but declared first to those in Damascus, then in Jerusalem and throughout all the region of Judea, and also to the Gentiles, that they should repent and turn to God, performing deeds in keeping with their repentance. For this reason, the Jews seized me in the temple

---
[1] sýmfytos (σύμφυτος, BDAG 6997).

and tried to kill me. (Acts 26:19–21)

Paul did not have a death wish in offering testimony in dangerous situations. He simply honored God rather than men. It was part of his witness to King Agrippa before going to Rome, where he later died around AD 64.

∞

Almighty Father,

All praise and honor, power and dominion, truth and justice are yours because at just the right time, Christ died for our sins (Rom 5:6) that in following his example we might have everlasting life.

Forgive our unwillingness to pay attention to nudges by the Holy Spirit to deal with our weaknesses and to follow your example.

Thank you that through the example of Jesus, we can live as you lived, make ourselves available to those around us, and die to our sins through confession and God's grace.

In the power of the Holy Spirit, open our eyes, unstop our ears, and grant us a willing heart to read your word, hear your message, and love as you do.

In Jesus' precious name, Amen.

Questions
1. Why do we care about Paul's journey of faith?
2. How many times does the book of Acts retell the story of Paul's conversion and what were the contexts?
3. What is the participationist theology that Paul wrote about?
4. What are some reasons Judaism and Christianity separated?

Primacy of Divinity

> *Whenever Moses went in before the LORD to speak with him,*
> *he would remove the veil, until he came out.*
> *And when he came out and told the people of Israel*
> *what he was commanded,*
> *the people of Israel would see the face of Moses,*
> *that the skin of Moses' face was shining.*
> *And Moses would put the veil over his face again,*
> *until he went in to speak with him.*
> (Exod 34:34–35)

Warner Sallmon painted one of the most recognizable portraits of Jesus called the "Head of Christ" in 1940. As a successful commercial artist and ad man, Sallmon marketed this image all over the world. While this image has recently come under attack for its portrayal of Jesus as a white European (House 2020), what stands out looking at the painting is its picturing of Jesus sporting "the glow." The glow is something missing from most postmodern renderings of Jesus, such as the cover art on this book, that focus on the humanity, not the divinity, of Christ.

The Preoccupation With Divinity

"The glow" alludes to the way that Moses' face radiated light after he met with God. In the New Testament, Jesus oozes light during the Transfiguration (Matt 17:1–8). The glow is a physical manifestation of the New Testament's preoccupation with the divinity of Christ. Consider the Apostle Paul's report on the resurrection:

> For I delivered to you as of first importance what I also received: that Christ died for our sins in accordance with the Scriptures, that he was buried, that he was raised on the third day in accordance with the Scriptures, and that he appeared to Cephas, then to the twelve. Then he appeared to more than five hundred brothers at one time, most of whom are still alive, though some have fallen asleep. Then he appeared to James, then to all the apostles. (1 Cor 15:3–7)

Paul never met the person of Jesus only the Risen Christ, but at least three additional reasons account for his preoccupation with divinity.

The first reason is that divinity is more topical than humanity. If you met the Son of God and were to tell your friends, what details would you focus on? Paul states clearly that the most important thing to know is that Christ died for our sins and has been resurrected—he is alive.

The second reason is because the resurrection was a public event. Paul reports that Jesus appeared to as many as five hundred brothers at one time, many of whom were still alive when he wrote to the Corinthians. This implies that Christ's divinity was beyond dispute for these eye witnesses, and it served as an exclamation mark for this teaching. Jesus' humanity was so obvious that it went without mention.

The third reason is that Paul wrote primarily to a gentile audience with a focus on pastoral and evangelistic objectives. A good leader was someone who focused on the things that we can all agree on, not the things that lead to strife. In this ministry context, we can all agree on objective ideas like divinity, priorities, and theology, while subjective ideas, like feelings, politics, and ethnic/cultural/gender concerns are harder to communicate and agree on. Jesus' ethnicity and appearance would not be a selling point with a gentile audience.

Ministry Application

Jesus is pictured as an emotionally intelligent person, but his personal appearance, friends, and family are only mentioned in passing. In our own ministry, our social position is something that we presumably use to communicate the Gospel more effectively, not something to draw attention to ourselves. It is one of those crowns that we lay at Jesus' feet (Rev 4:10).

∞

Beloved Lord Jesus,

All praise and honor, power and dominion, truth

and justice are yours because you came to us in the person of Jesus and sparkled among us.

Forgive us for our preoccupation with ourselves, ignoring your guidance, and living as if there were no tomorrow.

Thank you for dying on the cross that we might approach the Father as sons and daughters.

In the power of your Holy Spirit, help us to look up from our own preoccupations and participate in the lives of those around us.

In Jesus' precious name, Amen.

∞

Questions
1. How would you describe "the glow?"
2. What are three reasons that Paul's preoccupation with Christ's divinity makes sense?
3. According to Paul, what are the two most important things to know about the Risen Christ?
4. What experiences—good or bad—have you had that remind you of your social position? How have you used them to promote the Gospel?

Paul's Ministry Partners

> *Joseph, who was also called by the apostles Barnabas (which means son of encouragement), a Levite, a native of Cyprus, sold a field that belonged to him and brought the money and laid it at the apostles' feet.* (Acts 4:36–37)

Joseph of Cyprus, a Levite, is better known to Christians as Barnabas, a nickname given him by the Apostles. In Hebrew, Barnabas literally means son of the prophet, but Luke tells us that it means son of encouragement, a metaphorical inference (Acts 4:36).

Joseph made a substantial donation to the early church (Acts 4:37), which no doubt demonstrated serious encouragement. But the second time that Barnabas is mentioned, his encouragement takes an entirely different turn:

> And when he [the Apostle Paul] had come to Jerusalem, he attempted to join the disciples. And they were all afraid of him, for they did not believe that he was a disciple. But Barnabas took him and brought him to the apostles and declared to them how on the road he had seen the Lord, who spoke to him, and how at Damascus he had preached boldly in the name of Jesus. (Acts 9:26–27)

Bringing Paul to the Apostles took moxy—Paul had previously been a persecutor "ravaging the church" (Acts 8:3) and, out of fear, the Apostles shunned him.

Mentoring Beyond Words

But Barnabas did not stop with introductions. He actively mentored Paul in ministry. When the Apostles heard that the Antioch Church was growing, they sent Barnabas to investigate. Barnabas worked with the Antioch Church, and his ministry helped them grow. But Barnabas saw more potential:

> So Barnabas went to Tarsus to look for Saul, and when he had found him, he brought him to Antioch. For a whole year they met with the church and taught a great many people. And in Antioch the disciples were first called Christians. (Acts 11:25–26)

Antioch was one of the first century's most important churches, but more importantly this was where—thanks to Barnabas—Paul learned to be an evangelist. This opportunity arose after previously having been more-or-less exiled by the Apostles to his hometown in Tarsus.

It was in Antioch that Paul received his gentile commission: "The Holy Spirit said, Set apart for me Barnabas and Saul [Paul] for the work to which I have called them. Then after fasting and praying they laid their hands on them and sent them off." (Acts 13:2–3) This commission is attributed the Holy Spirit. Barnabas continued his work of mentoring Paul even during his first missionary trip.

Fruit of Mentoring

What if Barnabas had just tooted his own horn, ignored Paul's talents, and shunned him like everyone else? Petty, self-serving, and weak leadership is more typical than good mentoring in most organizations, not just the church.

Paul's evangelism established churches throughout Asia Minor into Greece all the way to Rome. He also personally wrote more than half the books of the New Testament (NT) and likely encouraged other authors to write NT books. These accomplishments helped form the foundation of the early church. None of them would have been done (or at least would have been delayed) had Barnabas not mentored Paul.

Mentee Becomes Mentor

Barnabas' influence is obvious in Paul's effort to continue the mentoring of many churches through his letters and many individuals, including Silvanus, Sosthenes, Timothy, and likely Titus, who are all mentioned. Timothy is mentioned four times as a co-author of a Pauline letter; Silvanus is mentioned twice. Paul likely mentored each of these colleagues and mentioned them in letter introductions because they served as messengers to bring the letters to the churches addressed. Titus, like Timothy, is addressed in a separate letter and mentioned many times but he is more a colleague of Paul than a mentee.

Even today, co-authorship often suggests a mentoring relationship. A professor, such as my father during his time at Purdue University, might co-author papers with his graduate students and lesser-known colleagues to lend them credibility and visibility in professional circles. Oftentimes, the students wrote the papers, which the professor edited. In Paul's case, his colleagues also may have served him as an amanuensis (or scribe), whose particular talent would be to legibly write in Greek using the least amount of parchment, which was expensive.

Paul's Influence on the Gospels

Two of Paul's ministry partners were also influential in their own right: Mark and Luke. Both traveled with Paul on his missionary journeys and both later authored Gospels (e.g. 2 Tim 4:11), even though not having been among the apostles.

Scholars believe that the Gospel of Mark was the

first Gospel to be written, because both Matthew and Luke display literary dependence on Mark's Gospel. Some believe that Mark's role in Paul's ministry was to recite the stories of Jesus, because Paul did not know the person of Jesus, only the Risen Christ. Mark had served as an amanuensis to the Apostle Peter, so he was well acquainted with these stories. Early written accounts of these stories are likely the source of the Q manuscript.

Outside of Paul's role as a mentor, he gave his ministry partners an audience for the stories of Jesus, something unique to humble leaders who don't feel obligated to talk all the time. While most of us tell colorful stories about the people we know, only the stories written down ordinarily pass the test of time. Paul's contribution to the preservation of the Jesus stories should not be underestimated.

∞

Most Merciful Father,

All praise and honor, power and dominion, truth and justice are yours, because you raise up charismatic leaders from the most unexpected of places and personally mentor us through your Holy Spirit. Be ever near.

Forgive us for overlooking the talents of the people

around us and rushing to speak when we should listen. Forgive our prideful ways.

Thank you for human mentors, such as Barnabas and Paul, who look beyond themselves to build up the church and strengthen newcomers in the faith. May we emulate their mentorship.

In the power of your Holy Spirit, raise up a new generation of leaders in your church who can speak with authority and live lives worthy of the faith that you have given them.

In Jesus' precious name, Amen.

∞

Questions
1. Who was Barnabas and what does his name mean in Hebrew?
2. How many of Paul's co-authors can you name?
3. What was special about Timothy?
4. How did Paul influence the writing of the Gospels?

Gospel Timing

That I may know him and the power of his resurrection, and may share his sufferings, becoming like him in his death, that by any means possible I may attain the resurrection from the dead.
(Phil 3:10–11)

Life is cloaked in the mystery of what has yet to be revealed. Uncertainty defines the experience of life. We buy insurance for our homes, our medical care, and care of our families—even our pets—in the face of an uncertain future. Uncertainty is woven into the fabric of life.

By contrast, the Gospels, like any obituary, record the life of Jesus, knowing the end of the story. Much like Paul knew that Jesus is divine, the Gospels begin with a resurrection subtext. This poses a serious problem for postmodern people who read the Gospels discounting Christ's divinity and presuming that Jesus' life unfolds more or less like our own, except without the uncertainty. The key claim of the New Testament (the divinity of Christ)—really the only reason to read it—is often treated as fiction.

The Pauline Path

Jesus' divinity was obvious to eyewitnesses of the resurrection and to Paul through his experience with the

Risen Christ. The implications of this divinity for faith were less obvious. Paul's journey after his conversion is summarized as:

> I did not immediately consult with anyone; nor did I go up to Jerusalem to those who were apostles before me, but I went away into Arabia, and returned again to Damascus. Then after three years I went up to Jerusalem to visit Cephas and remained with him fifteen days. (Gal 1:16–18)

This brief account of Paul's faith journey rings true because he was a highly intelligent and educated individual, and his transformation was profound. Many smart people cannot be told anything—they have to learn things for themselves. Today, three years of study sounds like earning a master's of divinity in seminary.

While the late writing of the Gospels is usually associated with the impending death of eyewitnesses, at least two points in Paul's writing suggests a theological reason to dial back and study Jesus' humanity. The first is summarized in the Philippians 3 passage cited at the beginning of the chapter. The second provides more detail:

> Do you not know that all of us who have been baptized into Christ Jesus were baptized into his death? We were buried therefore with him by baptism into death, in order that, just as Christ was raised from the dead by the glory of the Fa-

ther, we too might walk in newness of life. For if we have been united with him in a death like his, we shall certainly be united with him in a resurrection like his. (Rom 6:3–5)

The idea motivating both passages is the notion that Jesus' life, ministry, suffering, and death form a template for achieving resurrection and eternal life. What good is a template based on someone's life when their life has not been recorded?

Differing attitudes about the importance of the humanity of Jesus show up in comparing crosses and crucifixes. The crucifix with Jesus on it stresses Christ's suffering, while the cross absent Jesus focuses on the hope in resurrection.

Gospel Timing

If this template is God inspired, as the resurrection suggests, then knowing every detail of the template is theologically important. This theological imperative suggests why the Gospels followed, rather than proceeded, Paul's writing. One would normally expect an encomium (an obituary) to be written immediately following someone's death, not be delayed until decades later. Thus, it is correct to infer that Jesus' humanity, while not immediately important to eyewitnesses of the resurrection, became the key to understanding and living life under the new covenant in Christ.

∞

Beloved Lord Jesus,

All praise and honor, power and dominion, truth and justice are yours because you came to us as a child and lived among us as a righteous person to show us the path to salvation.

Forgive our hardened hearts, our stopped-up ears, our blinded eyes, and restless spirits that we might come to know you better.

Thank you for the witness of those who traveled before us and taught us to pay attention to both your humanity and your divinity.

In the power of your Holy Spirit, enter our hearts, unstop our ears, open our eyes, and teach us patience that we might learn and in turn teach others.

In Jesus' precious name, Amen.

∞

Questions
1. What is the role of divinity in drawing attention to Jesus' life and ministry?
2. What path does the Apostle Paul outline in attaining salvation?
3. What theological reason may have motivated the late composition of the Gospels?

THE GOSPELS

The Context

> *He will sit as a refiner and purifier of silver,*
> *and he will purify the sons of Levi*
> *and refine them like gold and silver,*
> *and they will bring offerings*
> *in righteousness to the LORD.*
> (Mal 3:3)

How do we see Jesus introduced in the Gospels? A story normally begins with the author outlining the context—the stage onto which the character steps. Typical questions arise:

1. Where and when does the story begin?
2. Does the context tell us more about characters or the author's self?
3. Does an inciting incident initiate a journey?
4. How does the main character interact with external circumstances and other characters? Is there growth or decline?

In Greek theater, the gods were mostly passive observers, not active participants, in human events, so Jesus is clearly different (Vanhoozer 2014, 20–21; Sayers 1941, 51).

The Gospel of Mark

Mark's gospel sets the stage for the others. Mark begins with Jesus being heralded by John the Baptist, the way a king's coming would be announced. This allusion to Malachi's messenger (Mal 3.1–3) is significant for three reasons. First, the messenger is an inciting incident. Life will never be the same again. Second, the refiner's fire is directed specifically at "the sons of Levi," which were the priestly class after Moses. Third, Malachi is a prophetic book, suggesting that Jesus' mission is an answer to prophecy.

Jesus is heralded by John, and then baptized in the wilderness. This setting is both physical and metaphorical, but this baptism is unnecessary for a sinless messiah. In the Matthew account, John asks Jesus why he is being baptized, and Jesus responds "to fulfill all righteousness." (Matt 3:15) The contextual answer is more interesting. Jesus' baptism serves as a commissioning service blessed by God himself. This blessing validates the unity and love within the godhead, but also suggests a kingly allusion:

> When he came up out of the water, immediately he saw the heavens being torn open and the Spirit descending on him like a dove. And a voice came from heaven, You are my beloved Son; with you I am well pleased. (Mark 1:10–11)

Mark describes this act as a "baptism of repentance for the forgiveness of sins" (Mark 1:4), but full-immersion baptism serves as a symbolic death and resurrection. In

Mark's post-resurrection context, Jesus' baptism serves a prophetic purpose that anticipates the crucifixion and resurrection.

The Gospel of Luke

Although John the Baptist is Jesus' cousin, missing in Mark's Gospel is the family context that we see in what Luke and Matthew picture for us. Luke's account is more personal, and many believe that Luke interviewed Jesus' mother, Mary, in preparing to write. R.C. Sproul (2005, 14) reports that Luke offers a much broader picture of the role of individuals, especially women, and the Holy Spirit in the early church.

The story of Zechariah and Elizabeth, the parents of John the Baptist, exemplifies his family context, yet their names are symbolic. Zechariah means *The Lord Remembers* and Elizabeth means *My God is an Oath* (Sproul 2005, 16,17). Again, we hear an allusion to Malachi in the words that angel speaks to Zechariah:

> Behold, I will send you Elijah the prophet before the great and awesome day of the LORD comes. And he will turn the hearts of fathers to their children and the hearts of children to their fathers, lest I come and strike the land with a decree of utter destruction. (Mal 4:5–6; See Luke 1:17)

Zechariah and Elizabeth are childless and advanced in age so the angel's talk about children must have stung, but the angel prophesied that they would have a son—John—and he would be the person of whom Elijah prophesied.

The angel later visited Mary, who went to visit her cousin Elizabeth. When they met. Elizabeth reported: "For behold, when the sound of your greeting came to my ears, the baby in my womb leaped for joy." (Luke 1:44)

The Gospel of Matthew

This personal, family account of Jesus' arrival in Luke contrasts with the conflict in Matthew's Gospel. Matthew introduces Jesus with a genealogy, sometimes called a king list, and a family context, but it comes in the context of a battle for political succession. Jesus is born, and King Herod almost immediately seeks to kill him, as an apparent contender for the throne. Jesus' earthly father Joseph is visited by an angel who warns him of the danger, and the Holy family slips out in the middle of the night. They flee initially to Egypt and, after Herod dies, to Nazareth.

For us, the Matthew context is overtly political, but the American church has more typically hurried through it quickly. The liturgy typically places the slaughter of innocents the week after Christmas when many people skip church and pastors take vacation—a liturgical sleight of hand. Fear and death are not themes that most people associate with Christmas, which is usually marketed as a season of joy.

However, angelic visitations and midnight journeys connect well with immigrant communities who have lived with persecution, corruption, and death, as has been the history in Central America. For such folks, spiritual warfare is a thin veil over daily life. For us, the Matthew account provides an important interpretative guide to the New Testament social context.

The Gospel of John

The Gospel of John begins with a philosophical interpretation of the creation account: "In the beginning was the Word, and the Word was with God, and the Word was God." (John 1:1) The words in Greek for "in the beginning" as the same as in Genesis 1:1 "In the beginning, God created the heavens and the earth." The implication is that the world itself was reborn in Christ. John's extended discourse on light (John 1:4–9) amplifies Genesis 1:3, and it suggests a strong focus on ethics in interpreting Jesus' life before a segue into the witness of John the Baptist.

Salvation History

In each of the Gospels, Jesus is introduced interpretatively within the context of salvation history. Even in Luke where this history begins in highly personal terms, the story of Zechariah and Elizabeth parallels the story of Abraham and Sarah in that both couples were elderly and, yet, had miracle babies (Gen 17:19-21; Luke 1:13). The echo of Hannah's song in Mary's Magnificat (Luke 1:46–55; 1 Sam 2:1–10) likewise places Jesus' life in an historical context far beyond the backroom of a carpenter's shop.

∞

Almighty Father,

All praise and honor, power and dominion, truth and justice are yours because you broke into salvation history and lived among us, giving our own lives context and meaning.

Forgive us for downplaying your role in our lives and neglecting the biblical witness.

We give thanks for your presence in our lives.

In the power of your Holy Spirit, be our guide, directing and leading us in all that we do.

In Jesus' precious name, Amen.

Questions
1. Which Gospel best touches your life in how it introduces the life of Jesus?
2. How is Matthew the most political Gospel?
3. What is a herald?
4. What does the term *salvation history* mean to you?

Jesus' Early Life

> *Where is he who has been born king of the Jews?*
> *For we saw his star when it rose*
> *and have come to worship him.*
> (Matt 2:2)

If we are to emulate Jesus' life, ministry, suffering, and death as a template for achieving resurrection and eternal life, then it is important to know who Jesus is. While we do not know much about Jesus' early life, what we do know from the Gospels of Matthew and Luke suggests that he was an historical person and that his birth stirred things up.

King of the Jews

The title *King of the Jews* given in Matthew 2.2 is reinforced in the genealogies given in Matthew 1 and Luke 3. The Matthew genealogy is given for Joseph, Jesus' legal father. Luke 3 follows the genealogy of Mary, Jesus' mother. R.C. Sproul (2005, 60) finds it important that Luke's genealogy starts with Adam, while Matthew's begins with Abraham, which suggests that Luke sees Jesus' mission to gentiles as foundational. Genealogies generally serve to legitimize claims of royal blood, but for our purposes they serve to reinforce a righteous lineage.[1]

---

[1] For a detailed discussion of the genealogies, see I. Howard Marshall (1978, 157–165).

Matthew's use of the title *King of the Jews* is immediately followed by: "When Herod the king heard this, he was troubled, and all Jerusalem with him." (Matt 2:3) For us, the trouble in understanding this passage arises in a weak translation of Magi as wise men (Matt 2:1). Magi were wise men, but they were also Zoroastrian priests and, as such, king-makers of the Parthian empire. We might usually expect that a Jewish baby would be blessed by a Jewish priest or rabbi, as when Luke records that Jesus was presented at the temple (Luke 2:12). Rome appointed Herod as king because he claimed that he could keep the peace with the Parthians, who were now telegraphing their dissatisfaction with Herod's rule by sending the Magi.[2]

The story of the Magi provides an explanation for Herod's reaction—the slaughter of innocents—and the reason why the Holy family left for Egypt in the middle of the night (Matt 2:13–18). Jesus posed a political threat to Herod and all of Jerusalem knew it. After Matthew presents Jesus' royal lineage, later Jesus demurs when Pilate

---

[2] The Magi appear unaware of the political implications of their trip when they visit Herod's palace. This suggests that they were either politically naive or set up to take the fall.

The Gospels – 129

asks him straight up—"Are you the King of Jews?" (Matt 27:11)

The Christian Family

An echo of the creation mandate can be found in the Christmas story. In Genesis we read: "God created man in his own image, in the image of God he created him; male and female he created them." (Gen. 1:27) Being created in God's image implies that life is sacred and has intrinsic value—the source of all human rights. The love and care demonstrated by Joseph and Mary in the birth narratives of Jesus in Matthew 1 and Luke 2 underscore this point. Long before Jesus suffered a painful, dishonorable death on a cross, he was born following an inconvenient pregnancy, had dirty diapers like the rest of us, and lived in poverty.

One of the defining characteristics of the Christian faith is honoring each individual, regardless of age, as being created in the image of God. The Apostle Paul's writing is clear: "There is neither Jew nor Greek, there is neither slave nor free, there is no male and female, for you are all one in Christ Jesus." (Gal 3:28) No ethnic group is better than any other; no economic class is better than any other; and no gender is better than any other. Paul goes on to extend his concept to the family:

> Children, obey your parents in the Lord, for this is right. Honor your father and mother (this is the first commandment with a promise), that it may go well with you and that you may live long in the land. Fathers, do not provoke your children to anger, but bring them up in the discipline and instruction of the Lord. (Eph 6:1–4)

Because we are all created in the image of God, no age group is better than any other. Neither a newborn, nor a senior standing at the gates of heaven is better than one another. Christians are to value life stages equally by honoring each stage, and by not clinging to any particular stage as if it were preferred.

While this discussion of age equality may seem to be a Pauline extrapolation, Paul would have been aware of Jesus' teaching on the importance of children:

> And they were bringing children to him that he might touch them, and the disciples rebuked them. But when Jesus saw it, he was indignant and said to them, Let the children come to me; do not hinder them, for to such belongs the kingdom of God. Truly, I say to you, whoever does not receive the kingdom of God like a child shall not enter it. (Mark 10:13–15)

In family systems theory, children are a barometer of the

emotional health of a family, which is likened to a household water system that fails at its weakest link. A child acting out may indicate that the parents are having marital problems (Friedman 1985, 21). Jesus' concern for humility and servant leadership are simply other applications of the same equality principle (Mark 10:43–44).

Theological implications follow from Jesus' humanity. The author of Hebrews writes:

> For we do not have a high priest who is unable to sympathize with our weaknesses, but one who in every respect has been tempted as we are, yet without sin. Let us then with confidence draw near to the throne of grace, that we may receive mercy and find grace to help in time of need." (Heb 4:15–16)

In other words, when we face Christ on the Day of Judgment, we will face a judge who understands our weaknesses and sin because he lived among us. If God is merely transcendent, then this experience would be absent. The helplessness of the baby Jesus underscores his humanity.

∞

Blessed Lord Jesus,

All praise and honor, power and dominion, truth and justice are yours because you came into this world from an inconvenient pregnancy and were born a helpless child to live as the image of God in human form.

Forgive us when we fail to care for those around us whose lives have intrinsic value as being created in the image of God, not market value that changes with circumstances.

Thank you for the gift of salvation in Jesus Christ.

In the power of the Holy Spirit, give us the willingness and strength to follow Jesus' example in life and ministry.

În Jesus' precious name, Amen.

∞

Questions
1. Why is it important that Luke's genealogy starts with Adam?
2. What is troubling about the visit of the Magi?
3. What is the link between the Christmas story and the creation accounts?
4. What theological point can you suggest from Jesus' helplessness as a baby?

The Lost Years

> *Every male who first opens the womb*
> *shall be called holy to the Lord*
> *and to offer a sacrifice according to what is said*
> *in the Law of the Lord,*
> *a pair of turtledoves, or two young pigeons.*
> *(Luke 2:23–24)*

The prophet Micah foretold the birth of Jesus with these words:

> But you, O Bethlehem Ephrathah, who are too little to be among the clans of Judah, from you shall come forth for me one who is to be ruler in Israel, whose coming forth is from of old, from ancient days. (Mic 5:2)

The Ancient of Days is a metaphorical name of God most often associated with Daniel 7, a prophecy of the rise and fall of many kingdoms. When King Herod asked his advisors where the Christ child would be born, this is the passage they referenced. No wonder Herod got upset.

Birth, Circumcision, and Purification

Jesus is to be born in Bethlehem, which means house of bread in Hebrew, of the tribe of Judah, fathered by the Holy Spirit. Jesus, the one who saves, who was born in the house of bread, later performs a miracle of feeding thousands by breaking bread, an allusion to the provision of manna by God himself during the desert wanderings.

Who wandered in the desert at the time of his birth? Shepherds. What is the symbolic message? With the birth of Jesus, the desert wandering of Israel is over.

Luke's account of Mary's purification after the circumcision of Jesus cited above makes an interesting allusion to the law of the firstborns:

> Behold, I have taken the Levites from among the people of Israel instead of every firstborn who opens the womb among the people of Israel. The Levites shall be mine, for all the firstborn are mine. On the day that I struck down all the firstborn in the land of Egypt, I consecrated for my own all the firstborn in Israel, both of man and of beast. They shall be mine: I am the LORD. (Num 3:12–13)

Moses referred to this law of the firstborns when he consecrated the tribe of Levi as priests. In a symbolic sense, the firstborn baby Jesus, as the refiner's fire who purifies the sons Levi, removed the need for the Levitical priesthood (Mal 3:3). Do you suppose anyone noticed?

Nazarene

Another point can be made concerning Jesus being described as "holy to the Lord." When Mark and Matthew refer to Jesus as a Nazarene (Mark 14:67; Matt 2:23), some see a double entendre and believe it is an allusion to Jesus assuming a Nazirite oath:

> He shall separate himself from wine and strong drink … All the days of his vow of separation, no razor shall touch his head. (Num 6:3–5)

The Old Testament allusion is usually associated with Samson, whose strength lay in his long hair (Jdg 16:17).

This Nazarene allusion may have motivated the many paintings of Jesus with a beard and long hair, and to this day, Christians are referred to as Nazoreans in Arabic. If Jesus took a Nazirite oath, it would explain why he was annoyed with his mother at the wedding of Cana (John 2:3–5). No Nazarene would want to associate with a wild party and alcohol.

This Nazarene interpretation is in tension with other passages, such as the parable of the brats:

> We played the flute for you, and you did not dance; we sang a dirge, and you did not mourn. For John came neither eating nor drinking, and they say, He has a demon. The Son of Man came eating and drinking, and they say, Look at him! A glutton and a drunkard, a friend of tax collectors and sinners! (Matt 11:17–19)

The implication is that the Son of Man, Jesus' title for himself, was not a Nazarene, like John, although he may have been at an earlier date.

Bar Mitzvah

Bar Mitzvah is Hebrew for *son of the law* and marks the transition into adulthood. For women, Jews now celebrate a *Bat Mitzvah*, which means *daughter of the law*. When I was twelve, I took a communicant's class and joined the church, taking communion for the first time.

The story of Jesus at the temple in Jerusalem when he was twelve is normally told focused on the parental panic on losing Jesus for three days in Jerusalem or on his statement: "Did you not know that I must be in my Father's house?" (Luke 2:49) In conservative circles, his submission to his parents may alternatively be the focus (Luke 2:51)

Carpenter's Son

Even today, it is assumed that a Jewish young person being initiated into the faith would learn Hebrew. Where did Jesus learn Hebrew and acquire a detailed knowledge of the scriptures? His questions for his teachers (Luke 2:46) and his reading of Isaiah 61 in his call sermon (Luke 4:18–19) suggest that he was fluent in Hebrew.

Today, Jewish young people may only learn enough Hebrew to pronoun the words, not to interpret them. In the first century, business got done in Greek and people normally spoke Aramaic, which suggests that Jesus was at least bilingual. Knowing Hebrew suggests that he was an educated man, which would be unusual for a carpenter's son. Hence, the surprise expressed by people hearing him speak in Nazareth (Matt 13:54–56).

Baptism

Each of the four Gospels associates Jesus with John the Baptist. This statement is also paraphrased in all four accounts: "I have baptized you with water, but he will baptize you with the Holy Spirit." (Mark 1:8) In Matthew, John the Baptist preaches that "the kingdom of heaven is at hand." (Matt 3:2). Jesus repeats this phrase and later instructs his disciples to repeat it (Matt 4:17, 10:7). For this reason, some people believe that Jesus was at some point a disciple of John the Baptist, which would perhaps answer the question of where Jesus learned to read Hebrew and studied scripture because John was a Levitical priest.

The Lost Years

The term *the lost years* refers to the many unanswered questions that have arisen with Jesus' life and education prior to his ministry. Inferences about this period are primarily drawn from generalizations from the context of Jewish life and our knowledge of scripture. While these generalizations argue from textual silence, the laconic nature of scripture encourages us to argue this way under the guide of the Holy Spirit and from a perspective of faith.

∞

Blessed Lord Jesus,

All praise and honor, power and dominion, truth and justice are yours, because you grew up much like us, lived, and worked among us.

Forgive our unwillingness to see your hand at work in those around us. Help us to forgive the weaknesses of others and in ourselves.

Thank you for your Holy Spirit, embodied in the church.

In the power of you Holy Spirit, draw us closer to you each and every day.

In Jesus' precious name, Amen.

∞

Questions
1. What are the two meanings of Nazarene?
2. Where was Jesus prophesied to be born?
3. What is the law of the firstborn?
4. What does Bethlehem mean in Hebrew?

Available, Ask, Articulate

> *If anyone says, I love God,*
> *and hates his brother, he is a liar;*
> *for he who does not love his brother*
> *whom he has seen*
> *cannot love God whom he has not seen.*
> *(1 John 4:20)*

If we follow the template outlined by the Apostle Paul, what is important to know about Jesus' life, ministry, death, and resurrection?

With that template in view, many interesting details of Jesus' public life fall away. We are not, for example, asked to emulate many aspects of his early life that have to do with his Jewish upbringing, although the church may practice traditions that parallel them. Baptism has replaced circumcision; forgiveness and generosity have substituted for temple sacrifices; sacrificial living has emulated his death. Christians have often found unique ways to participate in Jesus' life and ministry.

Still, many of Jesus' healings, miracles, and exorcisms are simply reported, but others follow a pattern that is worth highlighting. Consider this account of the healing of the blind man, Bartimaeus, near Jericho:

> And Jesus stopped and commanded him to be brought to him. And when he came near, he

asked him, What do you want me to do for you? He said, Lord, let me recover my sight. And Jesus said to him, Recover your sight; your faith has made you well. (Luke 18:40–42; also: Mark 10:46–52)

Jesus employs a three-way pattern: 1. He makes himself available to the man; 2. He asks the man what he can do; and 3. He interprets the healing. While many of Jesus' actions are simply reported, this healing is interesting because of what it teaches.

Availability

Jesus made himself available to people in a surprising way, often stopping what he is doing to attend to the needs of individuals. In Jericho, we are told that the blind man is initially begging and had to cry out for Jesus' attention. When he does, the people around him rebuked him. What does Jesus do? Jesus stops the parade and attends to the needs of the blind man, expressing a surprising willingness to be available.

Robert Wicks (2000, 39–40) sees our willingness to be open and available to others as an important segue to being open to God.

Ask

Ever since I was young, I have marveled as to why

Jesus asked Bartimaeus what he wanted him to do. Why would he ask a blind man if he wanted to be healed?

Being available to people is one thing, respecting them as individuals is another.

Not everyone who visits a doctor wants to be healed. A hypochondriac might just want attention; a single person might just seek an eligible partner; a poor person might just look for a handout. The answer to the question may seem obvious to you, but it may not be the answer sought. Jesus was respectful by seeking to affirm the value of the individual by asking the question. We are all created in the image of God, but do we act as if that were true when we interact with other people?

Articulate

Not all of Jesus' healings are in response to faith, as in the case of Bartimaeus. In the case of the widow of Nain whose son had died, the young man did nothing at all to deserve being resurrected. Jesus acted only out of compassion (Luke 7:11–15). In the case of the paralytic, the faith of his friends is noted and the man is healed: "But that you may know that the Son of Man has authority on earth to forgive sins." (Mark 2:10)

A cynic might argue that articulating the reason for a healing is simply a matter of spin-control, but the wider point is that miracles, healings, and signs need to be interpreted. Otherwise, the cynics will truly have the final word. As the Apostle Peter reported:

> In your hearts honor Christ the Lord as holy, always being prepared to make a defense to anyone who asks you for a reason for the hope that is in you; yet do it with gentleness and respect. (1 Pet 3:15)

We need to bear witness to God when we act out of faith because actions require interpretation.

∞

Almighty Father, Beloved Son, Spirit of Truth,

All praise and honor, power and dominion, truth and justice are yours, because you came into our world to teach, heal, and bear witness to the power and love of God.

Forgive our silence, our lack of faith, our unwillingness to bear witness to the truth of God.

Thank you for the testimony of Jesus who was available to the weak and needy, who asked about their desires, and articulated God's love in tangible ways.

In the power of the Holy Spirit, draw us to yourself. Open our hearts; illumine our minds; strengthen our hands in your service.

> In Jesus' name, Amen.

∞

Questions
1. How does the Apostle Paul's template help us interpret the Gospel?
2. Why is the story of the healing of Bartimaeus particularly interesting?
3. Why do healings, miracles, and signs need to be interpreted?
4. Why is availability a ministry priority?

Emotional Intelligence

> *Blessed are the poor in spirit,*
> *for theirs is the kingdom of heaven.*
> (Matt 5:3)

When you pick a Bible verse, pick a good one. In Jesus' call sermon and his Beatitudes, he highlights Isaiah 61:1–3.

Sermon on the Mount

Matthew 5 introduces Jesus' Sermon on the Mount, which is a commissioning service for the disciples. A commissioning or ordination service normally focuses on core teaching. The idea is to talk about the basic principles of service, because the commissioning service is the beginning of service, which mmost people remember vividly.

What does Jesus talk about? Jesus lists nine attributes of his followers: Anxiety, mourning, meekness, righteousness, mercy, purity, peacemaking, persecution, and being reviled. In view are the first three verses of Isaiah 61, sometimes associated with the Servants Songs of Isaiah (Lindsey 1985, 144). Jesus also references this passage in his call sermon in Luke 4. The attributes of God found in Exodus 34:6—mercy, grace, patience, love, and faithfulness—are also in view.

The first Greek word in these nine beatitudes[1] often translated as blessed or happy is better translated as honored, given the cultural context. Blessed is used as a legal term in the Old Testament, but Jesus works in the Sermon on the Mount to redefine culture where the translation as honor is preferred (Neyrey 1998, 164–166). When Jesus talks about turning the other cheek or loving your enemy, he is instructing his disciples to refuse to participant in the honor-shame culture of his time.

Honor-Shame Culture

In Christian culture, honor lies with behaviors other than picking fights to prove your dominance, machismo, or special worthiness. How else could you say honored are the meek? (Matt 5:5) Strength among followers of Christ lies in associating with everyday people and listening to them when fashion dictates something else. Jesus made himself available to invisible people, like Bartimaeus. What did the Pharisees complain? "Why does your teacher eat with tax collectors and sinners?" (Matt 9:11) Today, we would say that Jesus was socially conscious and emotionally intelligent.

---

[1] Makario (Μακάριοι, Matt 5:3).

Emotional Intelligence Teaching

If we are to emulate Jesus' life and teaching, practicing emotional intelligence is a good place to start, but how do we know that emotional intelligence is at the core of Jesus' teaching?

Daniel Coleman (1995, xxiii) cites Aristotle in defining emotional intelligence as "The rare skill to be angry with the right person, to the right degree, at the right time, for the right purpose, and in the right way." For Jesus, emotional intelligence lies in getting your heart in the right place. For example:

> You have heard that it was said, 'You shall not commit adultery. But I say to you that everyone who looks at a woman with lustful intent has already committed adultery with her in his heart. (Matt 5:27–28)

This focus on the heart differs totally from Coleman's focus on when and where to get angry. If we calm our own hearts, a world of conflict and nastiness just melts away. Active listening skills build on a calm heart (e.g. Savage 1996). This is the context within which Jesus advises us to love our enemies (Matt 5:44).

Cognitive Theory of Emotions

Theologian Jonathan Edwards (2009, 13), writing in

1746 about the effects of the Great Awakening, noted that both head and heart were necessarily involved in effective discipling. Thus, he coined the phrase "holy affections" to distinguish the marks of the work of the Spirit from other works and associated these holy affections directly with scripture. The only story of Jesus where he is explicitly described as getting angry occurred when he healed the man with the withered hand on the Sabbath because of the hardness of heart of the Pharisees (Mark 3:1–6).

Matthew Elliott (2006 46–47) outlined a cognitive theory of emotions arguing that "reason and emotion are interdependent," unlike the usual assumption that reason and emotion are separate. In other words, the cognitive theory states that we get emotional about the things that we believe strongly. Our emotions are neither random nor unexplained—they are not mere physiology. Elliott (2006, 53–54) writes "If the cognitive theory is correct, emotions become an integral part of our reason and our ethics" informing and reinforcing moral behavior.

Christian Culture's Demise

One consequence of the dismantlement of Christian culture going on today is the return to the honor-shame culture that predated the Christian Era and had been mostly sidelined in the modern period. The gang warfare in our cities is often about turf and drugs, but the core problem is that gang members cannot afford to lose face (and the implied revenue) in front of their peers. It is not about the cool tennis shoes or the gang colors so much as the respect those things represent. Enemy love, forgiveness, and honoring the attributes of God all work to move away from an honor-shame culture.

∞

Almighty Father,

All praise and honor, power and dominion, truth and justice are yours, because you loved us first while we were as yet unlovable and taught us to calm our hearts to make room in them for your Holy Spirit.

Forgive us for being quick to become angry, fighting over fashionable tennis shoes and other bobbles that decorate our ignorance. Help us to moderate our emotions following Jesus' example.

Thank you for the example of Jesus Christ, who taught us to love one another and to make room in our lives for you.

In the power of your Holy Spirit, build up the

church. Open our hearts, illumine our minds, strengthen our hands in your service.

> In Jesus' name, Amen.

∞

Questions
1. How do you define emotional intelligence?
2. Why is honored a better translation of *makario*?
3. What is your favorite quote from the Sermon on the Mount?
4. What does the cognitive theory of emotion suggest?

Scandalous Engagement

> *And immediately there was in their synagogue a man with an unclean spirit. And he cried out, what have you to do with us, Jesus of Nazareth? Have you come to destroy us? I know who you are—the Holy One of God." But Jesus rebuked him, saying, Be silent, and come out of him!*
> (Mark 1:23–25)

The first example of Jesus' healing ministry in Mark's Gospel is an exorcism, which suggests that he prioritized spiritual healing. In a literary sense, this demon heralds Jesus, announcing his identity, but how does this story advance the narrative? What does it tell us about Jesus' personality?

Jesus cares about individuals both in body and spirit. David Benner writes:

> Caring for souls is caring for people in ways that not only acknowledge them as persons but also engage and address them in the deepest and most profoundly human aspects of their lives. This is the reason for the priority of the spiritual and psychological aspects of the person's inner world in soul care. (Benner 1998, 23)

This focus on individuals and their care embodies the intrinsic value that we have being created in the image of God (Gen 1:27).

Spiritual Warfare

The idea of spiritual warfare is hinted at in the creation account when Satan tempts Adam and Eve, and God curses Satan, prophesying human redemption:

> I will put enmity between you and the woman, and between your offspring and her offspring; he shall bruise your head, and you shall bruise his heel. (Gen 3:15)

Jesus' ministry of exorcism accordingly hints that this redemption has begun.

A second interpretation is also possible. When Jesus confronts demons, the allusion may be to a Zoroastrian influence where the god, Ahura Mazda, and an evil spirit, Ahriman, are viewed as equals, an idea often described as Persian dualism. Other biblical echoes of Zoroastrianism appear in Moses' account of the burning bush (Exod 3:2)[1] and Matthew's account of Jesus' birth when he was visited by the Magi (Matt 2:1). Zoroastrianism is the oldest monotheistic religion.[2]

Today, Zoroastrianism is a minor sect centered in

---

[1] Chahārshanbe Suri چهارشنبه سوری is a Persian festival celebrated on the final Tuesday evening of the Persian solar year, the last Tuesday evening before Persian New Year (Nowruz). Persians celebrate this festival by jumping over fire.

[2] https://en.wikipedia.org/wiki/Zoroastrianism.

India, but in the first century it was the official religion of the Parthian (Persian) empire, Rome's greatest competitor. Jesus likely encountered many Zoroastrians during his travels that would be impressed by a rabbi able to drive out demons. It would show that God was more powerful than such demons, which is a more typical interpretation of Satan's status in the Old Testament as a servant of God (e.g. Job 1). In this context, we might view exorcism as a uniquely first-century type of gentile ministry.

Jesus clearly ministered to Samaritans (Luke 10:25–37; 17:11–17). It is not a stretch to suggest that he also reached out to Parthians that were likely found in any Middle Eastern bazaar. How do you suppose a Pharisee would react to a rabbi preaching both to Samaritans and Parthians?

Context of Jesus' Ministry

Jesus' practice of exorcism suggests someone willing to engage in the controversies of the day. Jesus did things considered scandalous by his peers, like healing the man with a withered hand on the Sabbath (Mark 3:1–6).

How does Jesus' scandalous engagement influence your perception of the image of God? Consider the alternative. What would have happened if God became a man and nobody noticed? Jesus engaged and radically changed the culture of his day.

∞

Almighty and most generous Father,

All praise and honor, power and dominion, truth and justice are yours, because you placed the healing of a man above the observance of decorum and did not leave him to suffer alone. Be ever near.

Forgive us when we look the other way, leaving people to struggle with their demons. Help us to confess our sins and move beyond them. Be ever near.

Thank you for the witness of scripture and being present in our lives. Be ever near.

In the power of the Holy Spirit, draw us to yourself. Open our hearts, illumine our minds, strengthen our hands in your service.

In Jesus' precious name, Amen.

∞

Question
1. What do we know about Zoroastrianism?
2. What is Jesus' first healing in Mark's Gospel?
3. What is the Hebrew concept of soul, and how does it differ from the Greek concept?
4. Why pay attention to introductions?

Jesus' Young Life

> *And Jesus, full of the Holy Spirit,*
> *returned from the Jordan*
> *and was led by the Spirit in the wilderness*
> *for forty days, being tempted by the devil.*
> (Luke 4:1–2)

*W*riting about the humanity of Jesus has been an obsession in the twentieth century because of the Enlightenment problem with the divinity of Christ. Much like Thomas Jefferson went through his Bible cutting out the miracles, we find ourselves scratching our heads at what remains. In his preface to his own effort at this task, E.P. Sanders (1993, xiii) writes:

> New Testament scholars spent several decades—from about 1910 to 1970—saying that we know somewhere between very little and virtually nothing about the historical Jesus ... My own view is that studying the gospels is extremely hard work.

My own Old Testament professor simply described scripture as laconic, giving us a bare minimum of detail, which allows the reader to fill in the gaps with their own knowledge and experience. This laconic characteristic of scripture allows each reader to paint their own picture of Jesus, which gives the text a timeless quality, but it also leaves room for doubt.

Temptations in the Desert

Consider the story of Jesus' temptation in the desert after his baptism. The devil offers three temptations: "Command this stone to become bread," "I will give all this authority and their glory," and "throw yourself down" (Luke 4:3, 6, 9). Jesus answers each temptation citing texts in Deuteronomy 8:3, 6:13, and 6:16—temptations facing the people of Israel during the desert wanderings.

Henri Nouwen (2002, 30, 53, 75) interprets these temptations as leadership challenges to be relevant, popular, and powerful, but the desert context and the scriptural citations allude to Jesus suffering the same fate as the nation of Israel prior to entering the Promised Land. The original Jewish audience would have heard these allusions as messianic claims.

A skeptical audience today would doubt their historicity, but the desert wanderings, much like Abraham's earlier travels, provided the context for the people of Israel to learn to depend on God. If you are a rabbi being hunted by the authorities and you want to disciple your followers, what template would you adopt? The narrative of Jesus' temptations provides an interesting segue to the synoptic Gospels record of Jesus traveling around Galilee preaching and teaching. What does that suggest about Jesus' leadership?

The Single Rabbi

One of the mysteries of the New Testament is what happened to Joseph, Jesus' human father. Another mystery is why we are never told about Jesus having a wife, something unusual for a rabbi. The two mysteries taken together suggest a common solution.

One clue is found in the crucifixion account, where we read:

> Standing by the cross of Jesus were his mother and his mother's sister, Mary the wife of Clopas, and Mary Magdalene. When Jesus saw his mother and the disciple whom he loved standing nearby, he said to his mother, Woman, behold, your son! Then he said to the disciple, Behold, your mother! And from that hour the disciple took her to his own home. (John 19:25–27)

In the age before TV dinners and microwaves, preparing meals was a time-consuming activity, requiring considerable skill. It is highly unlikely that Jesus (or any other working man) would live entirely alone.

If Joseph died while Jesus was a young man, Jesus likely assumed the role of caring for his mother and siblings, suggesting why he remained single. Another clue is found in Jesus' first miracle account at Cana:

> When the wine ran out, the mother of Jesus said to him, They have no wine. And Jesus said to her, Woman, what does this have to do with me? My hour has not yet come. His mother said to the servants, Do whatever he tells you. (John 2:3–5)

This interaction with his mother, Mary, reveals a close relationship, but it also suggests a coming-of-age story with Mary perhaps giving him permission to enter a new chapter in ministry. He already had disciples, but it would have been hard for him to take this step because it meant that Mary would have been deprived of his support. This transition may not have sat well with his siblings (Luke 8:20; Matt 12:46).

My own wedding-at-Cana experience involved a family push. In 2007, I had already visited a number of seminaries and begun preaching as an elder when my sister passed away. At that point, my father pushed me to offer the eulogy at both her church in Pennsylvania and my parent's church in Virginia, where she was interred. It was my first eulogy, the first time speaking at my parent's church, and the first time that my co-workers saw me in the pulpit. The following year, I entered seminary.

Sepphoris

Hypocrite is one word attributed to Jesus, and it may suggest where Jesus spent time as a young man. It appears frequently in his parables, such as:

> How can you say to your brother, Let me take the speck out of your eye, when there is the log in your own eye? You hypocrite, first take the log out of your own eye, and then you will see clearly to take the speck out of your brother's eye. (Matt 7:4–5)

Prior to Jesus, the Greek word *hypocrite* meant an actor, not someone obviously two-faced. Where did Jesus get exposed to Greek theatre? The answer is presumably Sepphoris, a Roman city within walking distance of Nazareth that was destroyed in 4 BC during a Galilean revolt after the death of Herod the Great (Sanders 1993, 102–103).

It is likely that Jesus, as the son of a carpenter, worked to rebuild the city as a young man (Thurman 1996, 18). In Sepphoris, Jesus likely learned Greek and got a front-row seat to the exercise of Roman power in the region—an obviously formative experience. By putting a new spin on the old word *hypocrite* the inference was likely veiled to those in easy earshot not familiar with the speaker.

∞

Almighty father,

All praise and honor, power and dominion, truth and justice are yours, because you lead us away from a life of sin and prepare us for heaven. Be ever near.

Forgive our selfish and self-serving ways, when we know how we should act, but choose not to. Be our guide out of the desert.

Thank you for gift of second chances, for an example of how life could be better, and for the assistance of spiritual friends.

In the power of your Holy Spirit, draw us to yourself. Open our hearts, illumine our minds, strengthen our hands in your service.

In Jesus' precious name, Amen.

∞

Questions
1. Why is the term *laconic* helpful in discussing scripture?
2. What did Jesus do from the cross?
3. What is common among the temptations Jesus faced in the desert?
4. Where is Sepphoris and why is it interesting?

Pastoral Care

> *The LORD passed before him and proclaimed,*
> *The LORD, the LORD, a God merciful*
> *and gracious, slow to anger,*
> *and abounding in steadfast love*
> *and faithfulness,*
> (Exod 34:6)

What is your favorite Bible verse? As a hospital chaplain, this was initially my go-to question for assessing a patient's spiritual maturity. If the person refused to answer, I knew they were at one end of the spectrum. If they cited a verse that I needed to look up, I knew they were at the other end of the spectrum. Most answered Psalm 23. On her death bed, my mother cited this verse: "You shall love the LORD your God with all your heart and with all your soul and with all your might." (Deut 6:5) At one point, my editor complained that I cited the verse above—Exodus 34:6—too frequently. In Jesus' pastoral ministry, he mirrored these five attributes of God.

Consider the words that Jesus shared with the woman caught in adultery:

> Has no one condemned you? She said, No one, Lord. And Jesus said, Neither do I condemn you; go, and from now on sin no more. (John 8:10–11)

Jesus looked beyond the woman that she was to see the

woman that she could be.

This pericope (brief story) is a direct application of grace, one of the five attributes of God. Scholars complain that this story did not originate in the Gospel of John, but no one disputes that it is an authentic story of Jesus.

Saint Augustine of Hippo

God set the pattern for pastoral care. As Augustine then confessed his sin to God in private, he writes:

> Such things I said, weeping in the most bitter sorrow of my heart. And suddenly I hear a voice from some nearby house, a boy's voice or a girl's voice, I do not know, but it was a sort of sing-song, repeated again and again, 'Take and read, take and read.' (Foley 2006, 169)

Augustine borrowed a book of scriptures from his friend, Alypius, and opened it randomly coming to this verse:

> Let us walk properly as in the daytime, not in orgies and drunkenness, not in sexual immorality and sensuality, not in quarreling and jealousy. (Rom 13:13)

Convicted immediately of his own sexual sin, he took this passage as a word from God to him personally and went to his mother to announce that he was a Christian (Foley 2006, 160).

It is sometimes said that Western Civilization began

with Augustine's *Confessions* because it highlighted God as concerned about the life of individuals, such as with the woman caught in adultery. Today, spiritual directors work specifically to assist their mentees in recognizing God's work in their lives (Barry 2004, 2). This critique of Western Civilization is ironic because Augustine was born and lived much of his life in Africa.

Born Again

The idea that God created each of us in his image (Gen 1:27) and actively intervenes in our lives is a Christian distinctive that is affirmed in Jesus' healings, exorcisms, and conversations with individuals, such as Nicodemus and the woman at the well. Nicodemus and the woman at the well represent opposite ends of the social continuum. Nicodemus is a first-century celebrity who came to Jesus at night, while the woman at the well is often described as a prostitute who came to Jesus in the heat of the day. Both individuals met Jesus personally, asked questions, and left changed people.

The conversation with Nicodemus was iconic:

> Rabbi, we know that you are a teacher come from God, for no one can do these signs that you do unless God is with him. Jesus answered him, Tru-

ly, truly, I say to you, unless one is born again he cannot see the kingdom of God. (John 3:2–3)

Being born again of the spirit implies a complete reorganization of one's life to make God your number-one priority, an allusion to the first Commandment: "You shall have no other gods before me." (Exod 20:3) The term *born again* literally reads *born from above* in the Greek.

Your number-one priority in life ranks above everything else. It becomes the yardstick of other things. If your job is your first priority, then you evaluate everything else against whether or not it advances your career. If your spouse is your first priority, then you evaluate everything else by your spouse's opinion of it. This ranking issue is simple logic, but it explains why being born again requires a radical shift in your spiritual outlook.

If anything other than God is your first priority, then you commit idolatry, breaking the second Commandment (Exod 20:4), which implies that God is much less important to you. By insisting that we need to be born again, Jesus is applying image theology where every aspect of our lives should point to God in whose image we have been created.

∞

Almighty Father,

All praise and honor, power and dominion, truth and justice are yours, because you insist that we be born again, centering our lives on you.

We confess that our lives are hardly spiritual and our priorities are often wrong, shifting, and self-serving. We are forever double-minded. Forgive our sin and focus us on your image.

Thank you for the witness of Jesus, who lived as a testimony to your mercy, grace, patience, love, and faithfulness, died on the cross for our sins, and rose from the dead that we might find hope in him.

In the power of your Holy Spirit, draw us to yourself. Open our hearts, illumine our minds, strengthen our hands in your service.

In Jesus' name, Amen.

∞

Questions
1. What is your favorite Bible verse and why?
2. What are the five attributes of God?
3. What Bible verse changed Augustine's life?
4. What does it mean to be born again? What does the Greek literally mean?

The Gospels –

Gethsemane

> *Father, if it be possible, let this cup pass from me;*
> *nevertheless, not as I will, but as you will.*
> (Matt 26:39)

Holding God as first priority in all things great and small is impossible. The temptations are too great, the time too short, and our energy too constraining. The Apostle Paul remarked: "For now we see in a mirror dimly, but then face to face. Now I know in part; then I shall know fully, even as I have been fully known." (1 Cor 13:12) The image of God is our guide, but we can neither fully comprehend it nor fully reflect it. Yet, Jesus in the Garden of Gethsemane offers us a guide on how to proceed faithfully.

Life is filled with pains great and small that confront us with a decision. Do we turn into the pain and hold a private pity party or do we turn to God and give it over to him? Jesus answered this question at Gethsemane: "Not as I will, but as you will." In this manner, we surrender our lives to God, raising the priority of God in our lives, one step at a time.

The Nature of Faith

Gethsemane reveals a view of faith that is seldom discussed. Faith is not once and for all, set and forget; it is contextual. The Apostle Paul alludes to this view of faith in Philippians:

> Therefore, my beloved, as you have always obeyed, so now, not only as in my presence but much more in my absence, work out your own salvation with fear and trembling, for it is God who works in you, both to will and to work for his good pleasure. (Phil 2:12–13)

Each painful experience in life gives us a choice—to move toward God or away from him. These choices establish our priorities. Is God our first priority or not? On sunny days, such choices are easy, but it's the painful choices that form our identity.

Holding the image of God before us is terribly important, much like the photograph of your family on your office desk, because it reminds us whom we love and why we work.

This context of faith implies that it is relational. We are willing to suffer for those we love, even if only out of duty, because our love gives life meaning. These faithful decisions are not market trades or investments in a heavenly future. We simply trust God to protect us, to remain with us, and to shelter us from fear in the midst of such pain. After the pain has passed, we appear faithful or not.

And God's grace resides with the fact that we do not always make good decisions. With each new painful decision, we remember God's faithfulness in the past. Our relationship with God is always a work in progress, as Paul suggests.

The Nature of Personality and Culture

Our personalities, our cultures are formed by the answer to this daily question because pain leaves an indelible mark on our souls and these marks add up. As human beings, we have a special relationship with pain. The behavioral response, psychologists tell us, is to do more of what brings joy and less of what causes pain. Our memories form a litany of answers to this question shaping our personalities and cultures into the image of God—or not.

In my own experience, it was relatively easy to accept Jesus as my savior. We all love to receive gifts. It was much harder to accept him as Lord of my life. We humans are a stubborn, willful race. We value our freedom, even if it means addiction, enslavement, and death. This is why progress in faith is so difficult, even for lifelong believers.

In this narcissistic era when we look around and see that all the toys in this life are broken, we all have family members and friends that simply cannot let go of their selfishness. This is why so many people die young from preventable illnesses, self-inflicted wounds, and addictions. Why else would life expectancy, fertility rates, and standards of living fall? These trends are more a measure of our spiritual health than our material wealth.

In turning to God in our pain and giving it over to him, we break the cycle of dysfunctional personalities and cultures. Why? We are prone to become addicted to things that bring momentary joy. Money, drugs, sex, and power all have the potential to trap us in dysfunction when they become our first priority. Giving our pains over to God allows the Holy Spirit to work in our lives to restore balance.

Image of God

How does this work? The image of God is a reference point in responding to pain. The question—what would Jesus do?—is not a trivial question. Balance allows us to learn the right lessons from our experiences, neither discounting our failures nor ignoring them. The church, especially small groups, provides an important forum for the work of the Holy Spirit in our daily struggles, offering us the support to learn the right lessons and move beyond our pain.

Over time, this process molds our personalities and changes our culture in the image of God. At Gethsemane, Jesus accepted the cross to die for our sins.

∞

Beloved Lord Jesus,

All praise and honor, power and dominion, truth and justice are yours, because you are strong enough to bear our infirmities, pains, and addictions for us when we ask. Be ever near.

Forgive us when we fail to reach out to you in our darkest hours. Be ever near.

Thank you for the witness that you gave to us during your time among us. Be near us now.

In the power of your Holy Spirit, draw us to yourself. Open our hearts, illumine our thoughts, strengthen our hands in your service.

For your name's sake, Amen.

∞

Questions
1. Why is our first priority special?
2. What is special about pain and the decisions we make as a consequence?
3. Why is the image of God important in our decisions?

Jesus' Final Hours

*So he asked them again, Whom do you seek?
And they said, Jesus of Nazareth. Jesus answered,
I told you that I am he. So, if you seek me,
let these men go.*
(John 18:7–8)

The Apostle's Creed summarizes Jesus' last days as: "He suffered under Pontius Pilate, was crucified, died, and was buried." Yet, the Gospels devote as much as third of their entire length to this narrow slice of Jesus' life. This is odd for an obituary because many funerals say nothing at all about a person's final days and death. What do these final days say about the person of Jesus that can serve as a template for us?

Transitions

Luke's Gospel commends much for us to remember about Jesus. What stands out about Jesus' trip to Jerusalem is the importance—even under threat of death—that he placed on celebrating the Passover with friends (Luke 22:15). Jesus' abstinence from alcohol is frequently cited (Luke 22:18). We all remember the words of institution:

> And he took bread, and when he had given thanks, he broke it and gave it to them, saying, This is my body, which is given for you. Do this in remembrance of me. And likewise the cup after they had eaten, saying, This cup that is

> poured out for you is the new covenant in my blood. (Luke 22:19–20)

Communion is an act of remembrance, but it also marks a transition—the end of Jesus' ministry and the beginning of his final suffering. Marking such transitions is an important communication device, both for us and for those around us, that something significant has changed.

Passover marks a three-way transition for the people of Israel: The exodus from Egypt, the desert wanderings, and the entrance into the Promised Land (Bridges 2003, 43). A hospital visit transitions from crisis to treatment to the question—what comes next? The treatment is formational; the question is inherently spiritual. Marking transitions gives us permission to speak into people's lives when they are truly listening.

Ad Hominem Attacks

Mark's description of Jesus' arrest, trial, and execution is well-known. One pericope in this narrative stands out:

> And Pilate asked him, Are you the King of the Jews? And he answered him, You have said so. And the chief priests accused him of many things. And Pilate again asked him, Have you no answer to make? See how many charges they bring against you. But Jesus made no further an-

swer, so that Pilate was amazed. (Mark 15:2–5)

Most commentaries on this snippet focus on Pilate's question—Are you the King of the Jews? Jesus simply responds to Pilate with Pilate's own assertion. After the chief priests badgered him with questions, Jesus makes no response and Pilate is amazed.

The principle behind Jesus' silence is that one cannot succeed alone in a defense against an ad hominem attack—an attack on your integrity. Someone must speak for you. This is why it is normally foolish to have a defendant defend himself or even offer evidence in court. Pilate gets it, and he is surprised that Jesus also gets it. A point-by-point rebuttal assumes that someone is listening and impartial, which is not the case here. Jesus is smart enough to be silent (Matt 5:38–39).

While Jesus' silence may seem like a footnote in the story of his trial, it poses insight into our own witnessing. We cannot afford to be passive observers when good people are falsely accused. We need to speak for them even if it comes at great cost to us personally. Part of our witnessing is defending those among us being subjected to unfair ad hominem attacks. It is simple justice and an effective form of witnessing where none is expected. Do you think someone you helped in this way will remember?

Straight Up

Each of the Gospel accounts of the crucifixion states that Jesus was offered sour wine. Only the Matthew amount offers more detail: "They offered him wine to drink, mixed with gall, but when he tasted it, he would not drink it." (Matt 27:34) Mark's Gospel describes it as myrrh (Mark 15:23). Jesus is offered the wine a second time in the Matthew account that enabled him to utter his final words (Matt 27:48–50). The composition of the gall (or myrrh) is in dispute, but the context suggests that it was offered as a sedative to dull the pain of crucifixion.

Jesus' refusal of the sour wine and gall (myrrh) suggests that he wanted to retain a clear head. Gall is mentioned twice in the Old Testament (Job 16:13; Lam 3:19) where its presence indicates a painful death is imminent. The only other mention of gall in the New Testament arises when Peter curses Simon the Magician who attempted to buy the Holy Spirit with money (Acts 8:23).

If Jesus sought to retain a clear head even on the cross, then we should endeavor to live daily life straight up.

Servant Leadership

The Gospel of John spends more time than the Synoptic Gospels on Jesus' last hours. John's account does not include the Last Supper communion account found in the others, but Jesus performs miracles of wine and bread that may function as a communion substitute, not for insiders but for outsiders. Only in John do we read:

> He laid aside his outer garments, and taking a towel, tied it around his waist. Then he poured water into a basin and began to wash the disciples' feet and to wipe them with the towel that was wrapped around him. (John 13:4–5)

By washing his disciples' feet, Jesus acted out his own humble teaching: "The greatest among you shall be your servant." (Matt 23:11)

When Jesus was arrested, he left quietly so that his disciples might go free (John 18:7–8). If we are to emulate the image of God that we see in Jesus, servant leadership is a good place to start.

∞

Beloved Savior.

All praise and honor, power and dominion, truth and justice are yours, because you modeled a life of service and celebrated sober leadership. Be ever near.

Forgive us when we cut in line and try to get ahead of others, ignoring your humble example. Help us to do better.

Thank you for the example of life unswayed by personal ambition, malice, or pain killers.

In the power of the Holy Spirit, draw us to yourself. Open our hearts, illumine our thoughts, strengthen our hands in your service. Keep your example ever in front of us.

In Jesus' precious name, Amen.

∞

Questions
1. Why are transitions and justice important in ministry?
2. Why was Pilate amazed by Jesus' defense?
3. Why is gall an interesting detail in Matthew's account of the crucifixion?
4. What example of servant leadership does John's Gospel report?

The Risen Christ

> *Jesus said to Simon Peter, Simon, son of John,*
> *do you love me more than these?*
> *He said to him, Yes, Lord; you know that I love you.*
> *He said to him, Feed my lambs.*
> (John 21:15)

The resurrection of Jesus Christ is the only reason that we even know who he was. What is the image of God that we get from the Risen Christ?

Faith, Evangelism, and Salvation

Mary Magdalene discovered the empty tomb. After everyone had a look and left, it was Mary who stayed behind by the tomb and wept (John 20:1–10). Mary's relationship with Jesus stands apart from that of other disciples.

All four Gospels report that the Risen Christ appeared first to Mary Magdalene (e.g. Mark 16:9). Jesus said: "Woman, why are you weeping?" She does not recognize him, so he asks a second time. Still, she does not recognize him, so he calls her by name, Mary, which gets her attention (John 20:13–16). Jesus then cautions her not to cling to him and asks her to report to the disciples.

That evening, Jesus appears to the disciples. After convincing them of who he was, he commissioned them:

> Jesus said to them again, Peace be with you. As the Father has sent me, even so I am sending you. And when he had said this, he breathed on them and said to them, Receive the Holy Spirit. If you forgive the sins of any, they are forgiven them; if you withhold forgiveness from any, it is withheld. (John 20:21–23)

Note the compassion that Jesus shows in these encounters. Jesus has physical scars, but not the emotional scars that one might expect for someone having been recently tortured.

Mark's account is more abbreviated:

> Afterward he appeared to the eleven themselves as they were reclining at table, and he rebuked them for their unbelief and hardness of heart, because they had not believed those who saw him after he had risen. And he said to them, Go into all the world and proclaim the gospel to the whole creation. Whoever believes and is baptized will be saved, but whoever does not believe will be condemned. (Mark 16:14–16)

Note the phrase: "He rebuked them for their unbelief and hardness of heart." This sounds like he was agitated because they did not believe Mary's account of the resurrection.

In Luke's account, two disciples traveling to Emmaus encounter Jesus on the road. They recount the events of Jesus' arrest, trial, and execution to him unaware of his identity. Jesus then "beginning with Moses and all the Prophets, he interpreted to them in all the Scriptures the things concerning himself" (Luke 24:27) They only recognize him in the breaking of bread (Luke 24:30–31). Note the seriousness that Jesus displays in discussing scripture.

The Thomas Incident

Thomas is listed as disciple in each of the Gospels, but it is primarily in John's Gospel that we learn of his character. Thomas follows Jesus to Jerusalem knowing that he may die (John 11:16). Despite his courage, he seeks to follow Jesus more fully (John 14:5). When Thomas missed Jesus' first appearance to the disciples, Jesus returns primarily to satisfy Thomas' desire to have proof of the resurrection:

> We have seen the Lord." But he said to them, "Unless I see in his hands the mark of the nails, and place my finger into the mark of the nails, and place my hand into his side, I will never believe. (John 20:25)

When Thomas sees Jesus, he forgets about the proof and declares: "My Lord and my God!" (John 20:28)

The image of God that Thomas' relationship with Jesus reveals is of a God unwilling to leave anyone behind, much like a Good Shepherd (John 10:11). Thomas' faith is first-hand, not inherited, courageous, not untested, genuine, not superficial, and Jesus meets him where he is at.

Not Seen in Resurrection

Jesus' mental state in resurrection is theologically important. Jesus was tortured to death only days prior to the resurrection—emotional scars are expected. Consider what happened when King Saul had the witch of Endor conjure up the Prophet Samuel—Samuel became disturbed at Saul's audacity and prophesied his impending death (1 Sam 28). The only prophecy that Jesus makes is during his restoration of Peter (John 21:18–19).

Theologically speaking, what if Jesus held a grudge against his disciples, especially Peter, for abandoning him in his hour of need? How would you feel about appearing before a judge who displayed such a grudge? Jesus' restoration of Peter in John 21 is an unexpected act of forgiveness, consistent with Jesus' prior teaching on forgiveness and reminiscent of Joseph's attitude towards his brothers, who had sold him into slavery (Gen 50:20).

If Jesus, like Joseph, needed time to sort through his thoughts before reconciling with his disciples, then this might explain why he met with Mary Magdalene first.

Jesus' relationship with Mary was qualitatively different from that of other disciples even if we don't know the nature of that relationship.

Also not seen in the resurrection accounts is any indication of dementia. One patient that I worked with in the Alzheimer's unit suffered severe dementia after her heart stopped for only eight minutes. Resurrection was clearly a recreation, not resuscitation, event because Jesus suffered no loss of mental capacity and retained no emotional scars.

Continuity

In each of these encounters with the Risen Christ, Jesus displays humility, compassion, and concern about salvation with those he meets. Jesus' pre- and post-resurrection teaching displays surprising continuity.

This continuity is obvious in Jesus' focus on evangelism. Each of the Gospels has an equivalent statement to John's: "As the Father has sent me, even so I am sending you." (John 20:21; also: Mark 16:15; Luke 24:47; Matt 28:19) But to those that would redact these statements from the Gospels, consider the healing of the demoniac found living in a graveyard, a kind of resurrection account. When the man is healed and begs to follow Jesus, Jesus tells him: "Go home to your friends and tell them how much the Lord has done for you, and how he has had mercy on you." (Mark 5:19; Luke 8:39) In effect, Jesus sends him on an evangelic journey, much like the Risen Christ sends us.

∞

Almighty Father,

All praise and honor, power and dominion, truth and justice are yours, because you sent Jesus of Nazareth to live, die, and be resurrected so that our sins might be forgiven and we can experience eternal life.

Forgive our willful personalities, our unwillingness to listen, and our outright rejection of salvation.

Thank you for the gift of forgiveness, the atonement for sin, and our redemption from Satan's grasp.

In the power of your Holy Spirit, remain with us in spite of our selfishness. Draw us to yourself. Open our hearts, illumine our thoughts, strengthen our hands in your service.

In Jesus' precious name, Amen.

∞

Questions
1. Who was the first person to meet the Risen Christ?
2. Why does Jesus greet his disciples with "peace be

with you"?
3. Why is it noteworthy that Jesus does not display emotional scars following the resurrection?
4. What does Jesus say after the resurrection?

CONCLUSIONS

Trinity

> *Go therefore and make disciples of call nations, baptizing them in the name of the Father and of the Son and of the Holy Spirit.*
> (Matt 28:19)

A discussion of the image of God in the person of Jesus would not be complete without talking about the Trinity.[1] While the Trinity is not fully articulated in scripture until the New Testament, God's self-disclosure as the Trinity appears from the beginning. (Chan 1998, 41; Bishop Dmitri 1980, 14–15) reported that Genesis 1 and 2 paint three pictures of God: God who is a mighty creator; God who meticulously attends to his creation; and God who walks with us like a friend.

Creator God

The first chapter in Genesis paints a picture of God as divine creator who calls the universe into being with words spoken over a period of seven days. While much is made of God as a sovereign, king of kings, the language here is not one of command, but of invitation: "Let there be." God is a gentle sovereign who rules by virtue of creative activity, not conquest, nor purchase, nor chance. In his first specific act of creation, God created light—an eth-

---

[1] An earlier version of this discussion of the Trinity also appears in Image and Illumination (Hiemstra 2023).

ical metaphor. (Gen 1:3)

The first verse offers a summary: "In the beginning, God created the heavens and the earth." (Gen 1:1) This one verse radically changed the perception of time and space. In the Ancient Near East, the time that mattered was day and night, and the seasons—spring, summer, fall, and winter—that controlled the cycles of agriculture. The space that mattered was the boundaries on a particular kingdom or empire. Here in this verse, God stands outside of time and space, creating both.

Everywhere that scientists have studied, the same laws of physics apply. The order and stability of the created universe testify to God's existence and sovereignty. Kurt Gödel, a twentieth-century Czech mathematician, is famous for his incompleteness theorem published in 1931. This theorem states that stability in any closed, logical system requires that at least one assumption be taken from outside that system. If creation is a closed, logical system (having only one set of physical laws suggests that it is) and exhibits stability, then it too must contain at least one external assumption. God, himself, fulfills that assumption. (Smith 2001, 89)

Holy Spirit

The second picture of God arises in Genesis 1:2, where God is pictured like a bird hovering over the waters. This avian image of the Holy Spirit appears in all four Gospels where the Holy Spirit descends in baptism on Jesus like a dove. (Matt 3:16, Mark 1:10, Luke 3:22, and John 1:32) Hovering requires time and effort, suggesting ongoing participation in and care for creation. The Bible speaks exhaustively about God's provision.

The Holy Spirit goes by a number of names and descriptions in scripture including:

- Spirit of the Lord (Jdg 3:10),
- Spirit of God (Matt 3:16),
- The Helper or Comforter (John 14:16),
- Spirit of Truth (John 14:17),
- Spirit of Life (Rom 8:2),
- God of Endurance and Encouragement (Rom 15:5),
- Spirit of the Living God (2 Cor 3:3),
- Spirit of Wisdom (Eph 1:17),
- Spirit of Jesus Christ (Phil 1:19),
- Eternal Spirit (Heb 9:14),
- Spirit of Glory (1 Pet 4:14), and

- Spirit of Prophecy. (Rev 19:10)

The variety of titles suggests that the Holy Spirit plays many roles and suggests a God of power who is anxious to confer many different spiritual gifts. (1 Cor 12:3–6) By empowering spiritual gifts, the Holy Spirit makes the Christian life, community, and mission service possible.

In the Gospel of John, Jesus describes the Holy Spirit saying: "But the Helper, the Holy Spirit, whom the Father will send in my name, he will teach you all things and bring to your remembrance all that I have said to you." (John 14:26) The Greek word for helper here transliterates as the paraclete, which also means advocate, intercessor, and mediator. (BDAG, 5591) The verbal form of paraclete also means to comfort, to encourage, console, and exhort. (BDAG, 5590) John 14:26 equates the paraclete to the Holy Spirit.

Although we frequently think of the Holy Spirit in highly personal terms, the Holy Spirit founded the church at Pentecost, as described in the Book of Acts. (Acts 2:2–4) The Holy Spirit provides spiritual gifts, sustains life, and makes communication with God possible.

Person of Jesus

The third picture of God appears in Genesis 2, which retells the story of creation in personal terms: Immanence means near. As a potter works with clay (Isa 64:8), God forms Adam and puts him in a garden where he walks and talks with him directly, an Old Testament allusion to Christ. Then he talks to Adam and directs him to give the animals names. And when Adam gets lonely, God creates Eve from Adam's rib or side—a place close to his heart.

Jesus' messianic role is highlighted in the discussion of Melchizedek in the Book of Hebrews. (Heb 5:5–6) Melchizedek was the king of Salem (later called Jerusalem), and he was also a priest. (Gen 14:18) In Hebrew, Melchizedek means righteous king, and some believe it is a title given to Shem, the righteous son of Noah. (Gen 9:28) Saying that Jesus is a priest of the order of Melchizedek expresses the idea that he is also a king. In Matthew 24:1–2, Jesus prophesied the destruction of the temple in Jerusalem, which occurred later in AD 70, confirming his prophetic role.

The Divine Dance

In our discussion of the image of God, the relationship between Father, Son, and Holy Spirit dominates other images. The Trinity demonstrates how to live harmoniously in diversity, an important example for individuals, for the family, and for community. In the early church, the term for his harmony was the Greek word *perichoresis* which means divine dance (Keller 2008, 21–15).

For individuals, the Trinity shows up in the writings of Freud, who talks about super ego, ego, and id as the three parts of our mind. While Freud, the atheist, would chide at the idea of this linkage, his student, Carl Jung, described the psychologist as a secular priest to whom you must confess your sins in order to obtain absolution. (Jung 1955, 241) Inner harmony is an objective in pastoral care and in therapy, another parallel to perichoresis. Disharmony is more typical of Freud's students, as in the writings of Herbert Marcuse (1974, xi), often hailed as the father of Cultural Marxism.

For the family, the Trinity poses a model for family life, where father, mother, and child abide in intimate unity. (Tennent 2020, 65) The assault on family life in collectivist ideologies is no accident because the state is jealous of competing influences, especially covenantal relationships reflecting divine presence. Today's deconstructionists likewise strongly denounce Christianity as both misogynistic and homophobic, and they specifically oppose traditional family life (e.g. Marcuse 1974, 36).

For the church community, the example of divine harmony has direct bearing. The Trinity could be thought of as the first small group with members doing all things together in harmony (Keller 2008, 213–26). Jesus taught about this harmony during the last hours of his life by delving deeply into the relationship between the father and son, as recorded in John's Gospel in chapters 13–17 (Fairbairn, 2009, 37).

Our relationship with the Triune God provides an important example of what a loving, well-functioning community looks like. Because our relationships shape our identities, each member of the Trinity contributes something different (Miner 2007, 116).

Image of Unity

Jesus taught: "By this all people will know that you are my disciples, if you have love for one another." (John 13:35) He encouraged the disciples to minister in pairs. (Luke 10:1) Shared ministry was not only a lesson in evangelism—it was a lesson in unity.

Jesus' remark at the report of the seventy-two disciples—"I saw Satan fall like lightning from heaven" (Luke 10:18)—should come as no surprise. Building on Peter's description of Satan as a lion (1 Pet 5:8) whose modus operandi is to prey on the weak and isolated, church unity protects us from satanic predation.

C.S. Lewis (1973, 10–11) gives an image of disunity when he pictures hell as a place where people move further and further apart. At its best, the church is a place like heaven where people move closer and closer together. The church's sense of community is the metaphorical return to Eden (Acts 2:42–45).

The Apostle Paul painted an image of unity when he likened the church to the body with many parts. He observed: "If the ear should say, Because I am not an eye, I do not belong to the body, that would not make it any less a part of the body." (1 Cor 12:16) We are all special and yet differ in the spiritual gifts that we bring to the church through the Holy Spirit. We celebrate the gifts of others because our unity is in Christ and Christ's mission, not in our idiosyncrasies and differences. This is why the ideal

Christian leader celebrates our shared identity in Christ, not in gender, race, or ethnicity.

∞

> Almighty Father, Beloved Son, Spirit of Truth,
>
> Blessed are you, father of creation, who hovers over us like a mother hen and who sent your son to die on a cross for our sins. Your majesty overshadows the earth and you have set your glory above the heavens. (Ps 8:1) May we share your blessings with everyone we meet.
>
> We confess that we are unworthy of your attentions, your parentage, and your provision. Forgive our trespasses, heal our wounds, and give us hearts only for you.
>
> We thank you for the sweet taste of your fruits, the aroma of your son's teaching, and the touch of our neighbors that share your love for us. Let us not forget our gratitude or wander from your gates.
>
> In the power of your Holy Spirit, separate us in humility, consecrate us in your service, and may we share Christ's aroma with all who will listen.
>
> In Jesus' precious name, Amen.

∞

Questions
1. Where do we see the Trinity in the Old Testament?
2. What are the three members of the Trinity and do

you understand them?
3. What is a Messiah? What three roles can a Messiah play?
4. What does perichoresis mean?
5. What is your favorite symbol of unity in the Bible?

The Template

> *And as Moses lifted up the serpent in the wilderness,*
> *so must the Son of Man be lifted up,*
> *(John 3:14)*

The Gospel of John alludes five times (John 3:14, 8:28, 12:32,34) to an obscure event that took place during Israel's desert wandering. It is also referenced during the ascension account in Acts 1:9:

> And the people spoke against God and against Moses, Why have you brought us up out of Egypt to die in the wilderness? For there is no food and no water, and we loathe this worthless food. Then the LORD sent fiery serpents among the people, and they bit the people, so that many people of Israel died. And the people came to Moses and said, We have sinned, for we have spoken against the LORD and against you. Pray to the LORD, that he take away the serpents from us. So Moses prayed for the people. And the LORD said to Moses, Make a fiery serpent and set it on a pole, and everyone who is bitten, when he sees it, shall live. (Num 21:5–8)

The snake-bite analogy is an apt analogy to the postmodern experience because we all live under penalty of death and our time on this earth is limited. What do you do when you find yourself surrounded by snake-bitten people who refuse to pray or even to look up?

The Apostle John's response is to gaze at the image of God in Jesus Christ, recognizing that others may not accept the advice and will willingly forgo salvation. While today many refuse the Gospel, this has not always been the case. Hudson Taylor (1987, 126–127), one of the first missionaries in mainland China, recounted a conversation with a Chinese man in 1857:

> A few nights after his conversion he asked how long this Gospel had been known in England. He was told that we had known it for some hundreds of years. 'What!' said he, amazed. 'Is it possible that for hundreds of years you have had the knowledge of these glad tidings in your possession, and have only now come to preach it to us? My father sought after the truth for more than twenty years, and died without finding it. Oh, why did you not come sooner?'

Today, more than one hundred and sixty years after Taylor's mission to China, there are more Christians in China than in all the Western countries that sent such missionaries. This observation is true both because of the huge Chinese population, but also because faith has declined in Western countries in the postmodern period.

The Transcendence Challenge

Postmodern people live in a materialist world, where the only things thought to exist are those that we can touch, taste, smell, hear, or see. Because God lies outside the physical universe, he is defined by the materialist not to exist. The materialist worldview works like an invisible dog fence to restrict our imagination. Postmodern people are transcendence-challenged making it hard to believe that Jesus is divine and easy to believe that he was just an exceptional person.

The rub arises because the New Testament focused more on Christ's divinity than on his humanity.

The idea that Jesus died on the cross to redeem us from sin is well-attested in the New Testament (e.g. Matt 1:21; 1 Thess 1:9–10; 1 Cor 15:3)—a doctrine that is often referred to as the atonement. The Apostle Paul explained the atonement as a reversal of Adam's original sin. Adam was sinless until he disobeyed God in the Garden of Eden; Jesus was sinless, but obeyed God even to the point of death on a cross. The resurrection credentialized Jesus as divine, making his sacrifice sufficient to reverse the curse of death brought about by the first Adam's sin. Only God himself can forgive sins because it requires reversal of a divine curse (e.g. Mark 2:7).

Paul's Key Role

The Apostle Paul lived and wrote his letters decades before the Gospels, and he focused on the divinity of Christ, because he only knew the Risen Christ. Paul's explanation of the mechanics of salvation may, however, have motivated interest in recording more details about Jesus' life and ministry:

> That I may know him and the power of his resurrection, and may share his sufferings, becoming like him in his death, that by any means possible I may attain the resurrection from the dead. (Phil 3:10–11)

Paul's participationary theology pointed to the need to record Jesus' life story, which was recorded after Paul's death in the Gospels. In other words, the image of God in the person of Jesus was needed if believers were to live into the salvation template that Paul articulated.[1]

Thus, a record of the resurrection was needed to credentialize Jesus' divinity and reverse the curse of death, but a record of Jesus' life was needed to assure salvation. Given this template, Paul could write:

> If you confess with your mouth that Jesus is Lord and believe in your heart that God raised him from the dead, you will be saved. (Rom 10:9)

Elsewhere Jesus said: "What comes out of the mouth pro-

---

[1] Paul's template appears like a mirror image of John's famous statement: "For God so loved the world, that he gave his only Son, that whoever believes in him should not perish but have eternal life." (John 3:16)

ceeds from the heart." (Matt 15:18) Because in the Hebrew worldview heart and mind are interdependent, Paul's statement is a Hebrew doublet, repeating the same idea in different words. Confessing Jesus as Lord is therefore only meaningful when words and actions are in concert (Jam 1:22–24).

∞

Almighty Father,

All praise and honor, power and dominion, truth and justice are yours, because Jesus was lifted up upon the cross and resurrected from the dead. Grant us your Holy Spirit.

Forgive us for our limited vision and unbelief. Grant us your Holy Spirit.

Thank you for the gifts of forgiveness and the possibility of salvation. Grant us your Holy Spirit.

In the power of your Holy Spirit, give us eyes that see and ears that hear. Awaken our faith and fortify our strength in your service.

In Jesus' precious name, Amen.

∞

Questions
1. What does the expression lifted up refer to?
2. Who was Hudson Taylor?

3. Why does materialism diminish faith?
4. Why is the Apostle Paul a key figure in the New Testament?

Image of God

> *The LORD passed before him and proclaimed,*
> *The LORD, the LORD, a God merciful and gracious,*
> *slow to anger, and abounding in steadfast love*
> *and faithfulness*
> (Exod 34:6)

A few years back, my Uncle John accompanied a delegation from the New York Council of Churches that visited with Hosni Mubarak President of Egypt to discuss the status of Coptics following a series of terrorist attacks (2011). During conversations with Islamic representatives, he was asked to explain the Trinity.

He asked them: "Do you believe that God is above us? Between us? Within us?"

They answered in each case: "Yes."

"Then, you understand the Trinity." He responded.

The image of God in the person of Jesus comes to us from eyewitnesses to his birth, life, ministry, suffering, and death, as recorded decades after the resurrection. It is analogous to trying to piece together an account of submariners lost at sea during World War II by interviewing retirees in a naval retirement home today who knew them back then (Jenna 2024). There is no doubt that they lived and died heroically, but the details may be sketchy due to the passage of time. In the case of Jesus of Nazareth, we have multiple accounts of his public appearances, conflicts, and healings. These accounts are contextualized by the times and literary use, mediated by prophesy, and shaped by their retelling. No other person in human history has received this much attention—not even close.

Our creation in the image of a Triune God is one of the true mysteries of the Christian faith. In Jesus, this mystery is much less mysterious. Our image of Jesus is flexible, but not infinitely malleable. Jesus is Isaiah's suffering servant (e.g. Isa 52:13–53:12). Suffering can take many forms, while service implies availability and hard work. Death on a cross is a gruesome way to illustrate a sacrificial life. Yet, even in suffering, death, and resurrection, Jesus remained consistently gracious and concerned about the well-being of his disciples (Exod 34:6).

Our image of God in the person of Jesus is clearly not all about me. Jesus is the Great I AM, not the Great ME. Our narcissistic age is dialectally opposed to the image of God in scripture. Much like the snake-bitten people surrounding Moses (Num 21:5–8), we need the image of God lifted up to remind us of who we are and in whose image we were created (John 3:14). Otherwise, our tendency is to fashion Jesus in our own image. As in the Apostle's Creed, this is why the early church worked to retell the Jesus story.

With our eyes on Jesus, temptations and trials are less likely to snare us and we can live a fuller life.

∞

Almighty Father, Beloved Son, Spirit of Truth,

All praise and honor, power and dominion, truth and justice are yours, because you created and sustain our universe, died on a cross to save us from our sins, and live within us, guiding and protecting us during uncertain times.

Forgive us for our many failings—things we've done and things we have left undone.

Thank you for your image, high and lifted up, to save us from temptation, to guide us in our relationships, and to sustain us when our strength fails us.

In the power of your Holy Spirit, draw us to yourself. Open our hearts, illumine our minds, strengthen our hands in your service.

In Jesus' precious name, Amen.

Questions
1. What are five attributes of God?
2. In what way is God's image flexible, but not malleable?
3. What is your favorite image of Jesus and why?
4. What does a sacrificial life look like?

SCRIPTURAL INDEX

OLD TESTAMENT

Genesis
1.................................187
1:1.................ix, 40, 47, 125, 188
1:2.......................................189
1:3..............................125, 188
1:3–4.......................................35
1:27..............................151, 163
1:27.......................................130
2..................................187, 191
2:16–17.....................................6
2:19................................33, 35
2:23...35
3...92
3:1...37
3:15......................ix, 21, 91, 152
9:28.......................................191
11:30.......................................85
12:1–3.....................................80
12:2...85
12:4..................................80, 85
12:7...85
12:11.......................................85
14:18.....................................191
15:9–17...................................81
16:1–8.....................................85
16:2...85
16:4–12...................................85
16:16.......................................86
17:5...81
17:10.......................................81
17:15–16.................................86
17:17.......................................86
17:19-21...............................126
21:11–21.................................87
22:1–2.....................................87
22:5–6.....................................88
22:10–12.................................88
22:15–17.................................89
25:12–18.................................87
28:12.......................................54
30:24.......................................92

(Genesis continued)
34:2...67
35:22.......................................67
37:28.......................................92
49:1–10...................................67
50:20...............................92, 180

Exodus
2:11–15...................................93
3:2...152
7:9–12.....................................93
20..79
20:3.................................49, 164
20:4.................................49, 164
28:41.......................................71
34:6.............viii, 145, 161, 203, 204
34:34–35...............................105

Leviticus
16:16.......................................75
19, 20.....................................57
25:25.......................................75
25:23–33.................................75

Numbers
3:12–13.................................135
6:3–5.....................................136
12:1...27
21:5–8..........................197, 204

Deuteronomy
6:5...161
8:3, 6:13, and 6:16...............156
30:1–3.....................................91

Joshua
1:2...66

Judges
3:10 189
6:1, 6:6, 6:15–16 94
6:25–27 95
7:25 94
16:17 136

Ruth
3:9,12, 4:1, 3, 6, 8,14 75

1 Samuel
2:1–10 126
16:1 72
28 .... 57, 180
28:7 57

2 Samuel
7:11–13 12

1 Kings
12:1 68
12:27–29 68
19:16 71

Ezra
1:1 12

Job
1 153
16:13 174
19:25 .... x, 75

Psalms
8:1 195
19:1–2 10
19:14 75
23 161
49:7–9 7
49:15 7
53:1 6
78:35 75
103 75

(Psalms continued)
105 11
110 12
115:3–8 49

Proverbs
23:11 75

Isaiah
1:1 72
6:1 74
9:6–7 71
11:1–2 13
11:1–4 72
40:28 51
41:14, 43:14, 44:6, 24, 47:4, 48:17,
    49:7, 26, 54:5, 8, 59:20, 60:16,
    63:16 75
42:1–9 .... 13, 72
42:6 78
42:6–7 78
43:1–3 11
43:1–4 74
49:1–13 72
50:4–11 73
52:13–53:12 .... 73, 204
53:3 13
53:5 74
53:12 7
61 .... 13, 137
61:1 x
61:1–2 65
64:8 191

Jeremiah
19:4–6 88
31:33 78
50:34 75

Lamentations
3:19 174

208 – *Image of God in the Person of Jesus*

Ezekiel
1:27–28 18
2:1 101

Daniel
7 134

Micah
5:2 134

Malachi
3:1–3 122
3:3 .... 121, 135
4:5–6 123

NEW TESTAMENT
Matthew
1 .... 12, 128, 130
1:21 .... 7, 65, 199
2:1 .... 129, 152
2:2 128
2:3 129
2:13–18 129
2:23 135
3:2 138
3:15 122
3:16 189
4:17 138
5 .... 13, 65, 145
5:1–10 x
5:3 145
5:5 146
5:21–22 83
5:21, 27, 33, 38, and 43 82
5:27–28 147
5:38–39 173
5:44 147
7:4–5 159
9:11 146
10:7 138
11:17–19 136
12:46 158
13:54–56 138
15:18 201
15:24 .... vii, x, 65, 68, 69
17:1–8 105
23:11 175
24:1–2 191
26:39 166
27:11 129
27:34 174
27:48–50 174
28:19 .... 181, 187

Mark
1:4 122
1:8 138
1:10 189
1:10–11 122

(Mark continued)
1:23–25	151
1:23-27	59
2:7	6, 199
2:10	142
3:1–6	148, 153
5:1	182
6:3	22
9:23–24	36
10:13–15	131
10:43–44	32
10:45	66
10:46–52	141
14:67	135
15:2–5	173
15:23	174
16:9	177
16:14–16	178
16:15	181

Luke
1:13	126
1:17	123
1:44	124
1:46–55	126
2	130
2:12	129
2:23–24	134
2:46, 2:49, 2:51	137
3	12, 24, 128
3:22	189
4	x, 13, 65, 145
4:1–2	155
4:3, 4:6, 4:9	156
4:18–19	137
6:43–44	58
7:11–15	142
8:20	158
8:39	182
10:1	194
10:18	194
10:25–37	67
17:11–17	67
18:18–23	16

(Luke continued)
18:40–42	141
22:15, 22:18	171
22:19–20	172
24:27	179
24:30–31	179
24:47	181

John
1:1	46, 125
1:4–9	125
1:32	189
1:4	71
1:51	54
2:3–5	136, 158
3:2–3	164
3:14	197, 204
3:16	200
4:4–30	66
4:23–24	68
4:25	71
4:25–26	67
4:29	68
8:10–11	161
8:28	197
10:10	37
10:11	179
11:16	179
12:32,34	197
13–17	193
13:4–5	175
13:35	193
14:5	179
14:16	189
14:17	189
14:26	190
18:7–8	171, 175
19:25–27	157
20:1–10	177
20:13–16	177
20:21	181
20:21–23	178
20:25, 20:28	179
21	180

(John continued)
21:15................................. 177
21:18–19........................... 180

Acts
1:8..................................... 16
1:9..................................... 197
1:21–22.............................. 19
1:23................................... 19
2:2–4................................. 190
2:22–23............................. xiii
2:41................................... xiii
2:42–45............................. 194
4:36................................... 109
4:36–37............................. 109
4:37................................... 109
5:34................................... 15
7.. 17, 75
7:35................................... 75
7:49–52............................. 17
7:58................................... 16
8:2–3................................. 16
8:3..................................... 109
8:4..................................... 17
8:23................................... 174
9:1-2.................................. 99
9:1–20............................... 15, 99
9:3–5................................. 18, 99
9:15–16............................. 15, 100
9:20, 9:24.......................... 17
9:26–27............................. 109
11:25–26........................... 110
13:2–3............................... 110
13:9................................... 99
18:24–28........................... 27
22:3................................... 15
22:4–21............................. 15, 99
22:10,22:17....................... 100
26:9–23............................. 15, 99
26:14................................. 100
26:16–18........................... 101
26:19–21........................... 102

Romans
6:3–5................................. 117
6:5..................................... 102
8:2..................................... 189
8:29................................... ix
10:9................................... 200
13:13................................. 44, 162
15:5................................... 189

1 Corinthians
12:3–6............................... 190
12:16................................. 194
13:12................................. 166
15:3................................... x, 7, 199
15:3–5............................... 46
15:3–7............................... 106
15:17................................. 7

2 Corinthians
1:21................................... 76
3:3..................................... 189
10:3–6............................... 38

Galatians
1:16–18............................. 116
3:28................................... 130
4:23–26............................. 87

Ephesians
1:17................................... 189
6:1–4................................. 13

Philippians
1:19................................... 189
2:12–13............................. 167
3:10–11............................. 102, 115, 200

1 Thessalonians
1:9–10............................... xi, 7, 199

Scriptural Index – 211

2 Timothy
4:11	112

Hebrews
2:2–3	26
3:16–19	28
4:15	28
4:15–16	132
5:5–6	191
7:22–24	26
9:14	189
11:17–18	85
11:17–19	89
11:37	72

James
1:22–24	201
J2:21	89

1 Peter
3:15	143
4:14	189
5:8	194

1 John
4:20	140

Revelation
1:8	3
12:14	23
19:10	190

REFERENCES

American Psychiatric Association (APA). 1994. *Diagnostic and Statistical Manual of Mental Disorders* (DSM-IV). Washington DC.

Bauer, Walter (BDAG). 2000. *A Greek-English Lexicon of the New Testament and Other Early Christian Literature.* 3rd ed. ed. de Frederick W. Danker. Chicago: University of Chicago Press. <BibleWorks. v .9.>.

Barry, William A. 2004. *Spiritual Direction and the Encounter with God: A Theological Inquiry.* New York: Paulist Press.

Benner, David G. 1998. *Care of Souls: Revisioning Christian Nurture and Counsel.* Grand Rapids: Baker Books.

Bishop Dmitri. 1980. *Orthodox Christian Teaching: An Introduction to the Orthodox Faith.* Syosset, New York: Orthodox Church in America.

Bridges, William. 2003. *Managing Transition: Making the Most of Change* (Orig pub 1991). Cambridge: Da Capo Press.

Brown, Peter. 2000. *Augustine of Hippo: A Biography* (Orig pub 1967). Berkeley: University of California Press.

Brown-Driver-Briggs-Gesenius (BDB).[1] 1905. *Hebrew-English Lexicon, unabridged*. References to BDB are taken from the software product BibleWorks, version 10.

Brueggemann, Walter. 2016. *Money and Possessions*. Interpretation series. Louisville: Westminster John Knox Press.

Butterfield, Rosaria Champagne. 2012. *The Secret Thoughts of an Unlikely Convert: An English Professor's Journey into Christian Faith*. Pittsburgh: Crown & Covenant Publications.

Calvin, John. 2006. *Institutes of the Christian Religion* (Orig Pub 1559). Edited by John T. McNeill. Translated by Ford Lewis Battles. Louisville, KY: Westminster John Knox Press.

Calvin, John. 2007. *Calvin's Bible Commentaries: Hebrews* (Orig pub 1847). Translated by John King. London, UK: Forgotten Books.

Chan, Simon. 1998. *Spiritual Theology: A Systemic Study of the Christian Life*. Downers Grove, IL: IVP Academic.

Cloud, Henry and John Townsend. 1992. *Boundaries: When to Say YES; When to Say NO; To Take Control of Your Life.* Grand Rapids: Zondervan.

Coleman, Daniel. 1995. *Emotional Intelligence.* New York: Bantam Books.

Edwards, Jonathan. 2009. *The Religious Affections* (orig pub 1746). Vancouver: Eremitical Press.

Elliott, Matthew A. 2006. *Faithful Feelings: Rethinking Emotion in the New Testament.* Grand Rapids: Kregel Academic and Professional.

Fairbairn, Donald. 2009. *Life in the Trinity: An Introduction to Theology with the Help of the Church Fathers.* Downers Grove: IVP Academic.

Faith Alive Christian Resources (FACR). 2013. *The Heidelberg Catechism.* Cited: 30 August 2013. Online: https://www.rca.org/sslpage.aspx?pid=372.

Foley, Michael P. [editor] 2006. *Augustine Confessions* (Orig Pub 397 AD). 2nd Edition. Translated by F. J. Sheed (1942). Indianapolis: Hackett Publishing Company, Inc.

Friedman, Edwin H. 1985. *Generation to Generation: Family Process in Church and Synagogue*. New York: Gilford Press.

Goleman, Daniel. 2006. *Emotional Intelligence: Why It Can Matter More than IQ*. New York: Bantam Books.

Graves, Robert. 1972. *Greek Gods and Heroes* (Orig Pub 1960). New York: Dell Publishers.

Guthrie, George H. 1998. *The NIV Application Commentary: Hebrews*. Grand Rapids: Zondervan.

Hecker, Jenna. 2024. "World War II submarine wreckage found off the coast of the Philippines: Wreckage discovery of the WWII submarine *USS Harder* has been confirmed by the US Navy." Accessed: 27 May 2024. Online: https://www.usatoday.com/videos/news/have-you-seen/2024/05/24/harder-wreckage-found-submarine-world-war/73835662007.

Hiemstra, Stephen W. 2023. I*mage and Illumination: A Study in Christian Anthropology*. Centreville, VA: T2Pneuma Publishers LLC.

Holmes, Michael W. 1998. *The NIV Application Commentary: 1 & 2 Thessalonians*. Grand Rapids: Zondervan.

House, Anna Swartwood. 2020. "The long history of how Jesus came to resemble a white European." *The Conversation.* Online: https://theconversation.com/the-long-history-of-how-jesus-came-to-resemble-a-white-european-142130. Cited: 27 February 2024.

Jenson, Robert W. 1973. *Story and Promise: A Brief Theology of the Gospel About Jesus.* Philadelphia: Fortress Press.

Jung, Carl G. 1955. *Modern Man in Search of a Soul* (Orig Pub 1933). Translated by W.S. Dell and Cary F. Baynes. New York: Harcourt, Inc.

Keller, Timothy. 2008. *The Reason for God: Belief in an Age of Skepticism.* New York: Dutton.

Lindsey, E. Duane. 1985. *The Servant Songs: A Study in Isaiah.* Chicago: Moody Press.

Kirkpatrick, Melanie. 2012. *Escape from North Korea: The Untold Story of Asia's Underground Railroad.* New York: Encounter Books.

Lewis, C. S. 1973. *The Great Divorce: A Dream* (Orig Pub 1946). New York: HarperOne.

Longfield, Bradley J. 1991. *The Presbyterian Controversy: Fundamentalists, Modernists, and Moderates.* New York: Oxford University Press.

MacNutt, Francis 2009. *Healing* (Orig Pub 1974). Notre Dame: Ave Maria Press.

McManus, Erwin Raphael. 2021. *The Genius of Jesus: The Man Who Changed Everything*. New York: Convergent.

Marcuse, Herbert. 1974. *Eros and Civilization: A Philosophical Inquiry into Freud* (Orig Pub 1955). Boston: Beacon Press.

Marshall, I. Howard. 1978. *The Gospel of Luke: A Commentary on the Greek Text*. New International Greek Testament Commentary. Grand Rapids: Eerdmans.

Miner, Maureen. 2007. "Back to the basics in attachment to God: Revisiting theory in light of theology." *Journal of Psychology and Theology*, 35(2), 112–22.

Murray, Andrew. 1996. *The Holiest of All*. Update Version. New Kensington, PA: Whitaker House.

Neyrey, Jerome H. 1998. *Honor and Shame in the Gospel of Matthew*. Louisville: Westminster John Knox Press.

Niehaus, Jeffrey J. 2014. *Biblical Theology: Volume 1: The Common Grace Covenants*. Bellingham, WA: Lexham Press.

Niehaus, Jeffrey J. 2017. *Biblical Theology: Volume 2: The Special Grace Covenants*. Bellingham, WA: Lexham Press.

Nouwen, Henri J.M. 2002. *In the Name of Jesus: Reflections on Christian Leadership*. New York: Crossroad Publishing Company.

Oswalt, John N. 2003. *The New NIV Application Commentary: Isaiah*. Grand Rapids: Zondervan.

Pass, Denise and Michelle Nietert. 2022. *Make Up Your Mind: Unlock Your Thoughts, Transform Your Life*. Nashville: Random House.

Presbyterian Church in the United States of America (PC USA). 1999. *The Constitution of the Presbyterian Church (U.S.A.)—Part I: Book of Confession*. Louisville, KY: Office of the General Assembly.

Sanders, E.P. 1977. *Paul and Palestinian Judaism: A Comparison of Patterns of Religion*. Philadelphia: Fortress Press.

Sanders, E.P. 1993. *The Historical Figure of Jesus*. London: Penguin Books.

Savage, John. 1996. *Listening & Caring Skills: A Guide for Groups and Leaders*. Nashville: Abingdon Press.

Sayers, Dorothy. 1941. *The Mind of the Maker*. New York: HarperCollins.

Schaefer, Jack. 2013. *Shane* (Orig Pub 1948). New York: Houghton Mifflin Harcourt.

Smith, Houston. 2001. *Why Religion Matters: The Fate of the Human Spirit in an Age of Disbelief*. San Francisco: Harper.

Sproul, R.C. 2005. *A Walk with God: An Exposition of Luke's Gospel*. Great Britain: Christian Focus Publications.

Strobel, Lee. 2005. *The Case for Christmas: A Journalist Investigates the Identity of the Child in the Manger*. Grand Rapids: Zondervan.

Taylor, J. Hudson. 1987. *Autobiography of a Man Who Brought the Gospel to China* (1832–1905). Minneapolis: Bethany House Publishers.

Tennant, Carolyn. 2016. *Catch the Wind of the Spirit: How the 5 Ministry Gifts Can Transform Your Church*. Springfield, MA: Vital Resources.

Thurman, Howard. 1996. *Jesus and the Disinherited* (Orig Pub 1949). Boston: Beacon Press.

Vanhoozer, Kevin J. 1998. *Is There Meaning in This Text? The Bible, The Reader, and the Morality of Literary Knowledge.* Grand Rapids: Zondervan.

Vanhoozer, Kevin J. 2014. *Faith Speaking Understanding: Performing the Drama of Doctrine.* Louisville: Westminster John Knox Press.

Wicks, Robert. 2000. *Availability: The Spiritual Joy of Helping Others.* New York: Crossroad Publishing Company.

ABOUT

*A*uthor Stephen W. Hiemstra lives in Centreville, Virginia with Maryam, his wife of more than thirty-five years. They have three grown children.

Stephen worked as an economist for twenty-seven years in more than five federal agencies, where he published numerous government studies, magazine articles, and book reviews. Check WorldCat.org for a complete listing of volumes available in a library near you.

Stephen has published a six-book, Christian spirituality series. He wrote his first book, *A Christian Guide to Spirituality* in 2014. In 2016, he wrote a second book, *Life in Tension*. In 2017, he published a memoir, *Called Along the Way*. In 2019, he published *Simple Faith*. In 2020, he published *Living in Christ*. His sixth book—*Image and Illumination*—was published in 2023.

In 2023, he began his Image of God series with the publication of *Image of God in the Parables* (2023) and *Image of the Holy Spirit and the Church* (2023). *Image of God in the Person of Jesus* (2024) completes this series.

Two books from his Christian spirituality series are available in Spanish: *Una Guía Cristiana a la Espiritualidad*

(2015) and *Vida en Tensión* (2021). He also published his first book in German: *Ein Christlicher Leitfaden zur Spiritualität* (2022).

In 2021, he published his debut novella, *Masquerade*, and rewrote it as a screenplay under the title: *Brandishing the Blue*. In 2023, he published a sequel, *The Detour*, and adapted it as a screenplay. In 2024, he published another sequel, *Christmas in Havana*, which has also been adapted as a screenplay.

Stephen published his first hardcover book, *Everyday Prayers for Everyday People* (2018). He also published an ebook compilation book, *Spiritual Trilogy*, that year.

Stephen has a Masters of Divinity (MDiv, 2013) from Gordon-Conwell Theological Seminary in Charlotte, North Carolina. His doctorate (Ph.D., 1985) is in agricultural economics from Michigan State University. He studied in Puerto Rico and in Germany and speaks Spanish and German.

Correspond with Stephen at T2Pneuma@gmail.com or follow his blog at http://www.T2Pneuma.net.

If you enjoyed *Image of God in the Person of Jesus*, please post a review online.

www.ingramcontent.com/pod-product-compliance
Lightning Source LLC
Chambersburg PA
CBHW070133080526
44586CB00015B/1668